Back to the Boy

# Back to the Boy

## JAMES ARTHUR

HODDER &
STOUGHTON

First published in Great Britain in 2017 by Hodder & Stoughton
An Hachette UK company

1

Copyright © James Arthur 2017

A CIP catalogue record for this title is available from the British Library

ISBN 9781473665880
eBook ISBN 9781473665859

Typeset in Sabon MT by Hewer Text UK Ltd, Edinburgh
Printed and bound Clays Ltd, St Ives plc

Hodder & Stoughton policy is to use papers that are natural, renewable
and recyclable products and made from wood grown in sustainable
forests. The logging and manufacturing processes are expected to
conform to the environmental regulations of the country of origin.

Hodder & Stoughton Ltd
Carmelite House
50 Victoria Embankment
London EC4Y 0DZ

www.hodder.co.uk

To all my family, including my loved ones who are no longer here, and to anyone who has ever suffered from mental health issues.

# PREFACE

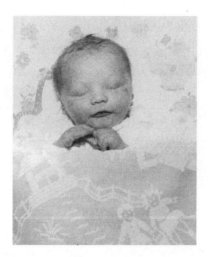

'I'm so sick. I'm giving up here. I'm losing my battle with depression. I'm crying. I've had enough. This is it. I'm not fighting. I need to go to rehab. I can't do it anymore. I'm sick. Babe, I'm crying. This is not me. All I can think about is curling into a ball. I hate myself. My mind is broken. I feel so sick. I'm scared of dying all the time. I'm permanently wired into my chest. I can't do it anymore. It has well and truly beaten me. I don't know what to do.'

This is a text message I sent in June 2014 to Jess, my girl-friend at the time.

I had locked myself in the bedroom of my flat in Chiswick and she was on her way over, scared of what I might do.

'Since when has it been unbearable?'

'Since after we spoke last night. Since forever. I've always felt like this. I hate myself. I'm so sick. I want to collapse. I've finally realised I'm an addict. I'm tired of fighting it now. It's beaten me. I don't enjoy life anymore. I don't want to cope. I want to be happy. I want to be healthy.'

I refused to unlock the door and Jess lay in the hallway outside the bedroom all night long, trying to talk me round, frightened I might kill myself.

I was so done with the panic attacks. I was so afraid of them and I couldn't work out what the point of life was. Why was I even here? My purpose had gone and I could not see it ever coming back. There was nothing at all in my future. I had no hope.

I couldn't accept that the highest point of my life was winning *The X Factor* eighteen months earlier, and having one hit single, 'Impossible'. Now that wasn't just the name of the song; the word described the implausibly calamitous course my career had taken since then.

I'd gone from making the most successful *X Factor* single ever, and selling over a million copies, to suffering a devastating fall from grace. I'd made stupid mistakes and failed spectacularly to deal with the pressures of fame. My behaviour had led to me being dropped by Simon Cowell's record label, Syco, and now I was a national joke; the loser and misfit and oddball I'd always known I was, ever since I was a boy. Ruinously, my career had crashed and burned at such breakneck speed I was already featuring in those 'Where are they now?' articles.

*Where am I now?*

I was on the edge, riddled with fear and self-loathing, panicking and crumbling under the agony of the deepest depression I'd ever experienced. There was no way I could ever claw myself back to sanity, let alone success.

'It seems James is self-destructing,' one tabloid newspaper commented.

This was as close to the truth as anyone got. I *was* self-destructing, but what nobody knew was just how serious and deep-rooted my mental health problems were, and why and how they were leading me to behave this way.

It has taken me three years to feel more comfortable in my own skin, and ready and able to explain the demons inside my head and how I have learned to cope with them.

I could not write this book without explaining my childhood. Nothing that has happened in my adult life makes much sense if you don't know what life was like for me growing up. I have to go back to the boy, because he can tell you a lot more than I can.

I'm grateful to my family, and particularly my mum and dad, Shirley and Neil, for supporting me in telling my story truthfully. Mam has been honest about her own mental health problems and the impact they had on me when she was too ill to defeat them and be there for me, as my real mum.

Most people only get one shot at the rags-to-riches fairy tale. Everybody wrote me off, including myself, and to have a second chance and to come back bigger and better is something I'm so proud of, and unbelievably thankful for.

I hope my story can help anybody who is struggling with mental health issues, and I hope it will inspire anyone who ever wanted to reach for the stars.

# CHAPTER ONE

*Normal? But I'm not normal. I've never
been normal. Nothing about my life
or the situation I'm in is normal*

My heart was beating out of my chest. *Please, no. Not this
again. Not here, not now.* It was too late. I couldn't stop it. I
began pacing the room, trying to breathe normally but gasping
and struggling to catch every single breath. I wanted to crawl
the walls, do anything I could to escape this room, this feeling,
this utter terror that I couldn't breathe and I was going to die.

I was about to have a heart attack, I was certain of that. I had all the symptoms of an impending heart attack and I was fighting for my life. The fear of what was about to happen to me made my breathing worse, and the more I tried to take a breath the more it felt like I was suffocating.

I couldn't escape. There was nowhere to go and no way out of this situation. I was trapped by my body. I was seizing up, and I had absolutely no control over what was happening. Now my face was numb, my left arm was dead and I had pins and needles prickling me, all over. My heart was pounding so hard it was definitely going to explode; I was losing the fight, for sure.

*This is it, the end. I'm having a massive heart attack. My heart is going to burst right out of my chest and I'm going to die, right here, in the* X Factor *studios.*

I saw flashes of light, sparks of fear and terror that pierced my brain as I patrolled around in circles, clutching my chest. People were laughing; I could hear them, in my head. There were voices I didn't recognise and high-pitched noises, and all the time the thudding of my heart was getting louder and threatening to blow me apart. I was aching all over with tension and my lungs were smashing into my ribs. My heart-beat was reverberating around my skull, making my ears throb and my mind bend with pain, and all the time people were laughing at me, laughing like demons.

Every breath was getting harder to take. My throat was so tight. It was refusing to let enough air in and there was nothing whatsoever I could do about it.

Then it happened. I saw myself falling and then there I was, lying motionless on the floor. I had dropped dead in front of myself. I could see my corpse, and the image was so shocking and vivid it made something snap in my head. This was crazy and terrifying and just off-the-scale horrific. I had to do something. I had to try to take control. I had to call for help or this really was the end of me.

*Someone please call me an ambulance. I need an ambulance, right now. I'm having a heart attack. I'm going to die.*

I hoped, desperately, that it wasn't too late. Now there were people everywhere, all around me, and all around my dead body on the floor. It was pandemonium, and I had no idea what was real and what wasn't. I felt completely crazy and totally confused. I didn't know what was happening to either my mind or my body. Whatever it was, this wasn't normal, no way. Something was very wrong, and it was very, very frightening.

*Just try to breathe. Breathe. Breathe. Keep breathing, because if you don't your heart will explode and you will die.*

The paramedics rushed in, wearing familiar, fluorescent jackets, carrying equipment I knew so well and saying things I'd heard before. It was like watching a re-run of a drama you've seen a hundred times already, yet I couldn't remember how it ended. The uncertainty gripped me and I could hear voices through the chaos. There were security staff and studio crew all around and I could hear people questioning whether I'd had a fit or an asthma attack.

*Take a breath. Keep breathing. Take deep breaths. The air is not getting through. This is it. This where it ends. It can't be. Just breathe, just breathe.*

Nicole Scherzinger, my mentor, was looking worried and offering words of comfort. So was Rylan Clark, my roommate during the live shows. The paramedics were checking my blood pressure, my pulse, my heart. I wanted them to hurry up, to stop my heart attack before it was too late.

'You're not having a heart attack, James.'

The relief flooded me.

'Everything is going to be OK. It's an anxiety attack. You're doing well. You're coming out of it now.'

I didn't need to go to hospital. I wasn't dying, and I wasn't dead on the floor. I'd had a severe panic attack, and now, at last, I was breathing a bit better, thanks to the reassuring words of the paramedic. I just needed to stay calm and keep breathing and everything would soon be back to normal.

*Normal? But I'm not normal. I've never been normal. Nothing about my life or the situation I'm in is normal.*

I went back to my hotel room to rest and I reflected on what had happened. Earlier that night I'd performed Mary J. Blige's 'No More Drama', in week two of the 2012 *X Factor* live shows. 'No More Drama'. The irony of the song choice wasn't lost on me. I'd created a whole lot of drama, and what was going to happen now? I wanted to run away but I couldn't, not now. I'd fought too hard for this.

When I was a boy I'd picture myself standing on a stage. I'd see myself very clearly, performing to an audience, singing and playing guitar and sounding good. The vision I had always seemed so real, and I truly believed it was going to come to life for me when I was older. My only other dream was to play for Middlesbrough FC, but I knew that this was just a pipe dream and wouldn't come true. It was always different with music. I had no doubt; music was my destiny.

I was in my early twenties when I finally started to acknowledge that maybe it wasn't going to happen for me after all, at least not the way I wanted it to. I'd been through a lot of traumatic events and I'd been trying to make it as a singer for years and years. The odds were stacked against me. I probably wasn't going to be signed up by a music producer who heard me playing a gig at a pub in Middlesbrough. A fairy godmother was not going to drop out of the sky and give me the money I needed to make demos and promote myself outside the North-East of England. The music I put out online was not going to go viral and land me the record deal I craved.

Then – bang – out of nowhere, here I was, on *The X Factor*. I was on the cusp of really making a career out of my voice and my music, and suddenly my childhood dream was within touching distance. I'd come this far, and there was no way I could walk away now. I knew that in theory, but there were voices in my head that told me otherwise.

*What the hell were you thinking? You're a loser. You always have been. You're a weirdo. This is the end of the road, James. Give it up, oddball. Nobody wants you here. Nobody will miss you. Go back to obscurity, where you belong.*

'What are you looking at, weirdo?'

It was a lad at my primary school – Ings Farm in Redcar – taunting me because my right eye was really turned in, making it look like I was 'bong-eyed' or 'cross-eyed', as he and some of the other kids said.

I was five or six years old and the bully's words did a lot of damage. He was making out he couldn't tell what I was looking at, because my right eye was pointing the wrong way. I felt so self-conscious and I turned my head away, stinging with humiliation.

My eye had turned in ever since I'd had an accident a few years earlier, when I was playing at home one day with my big sister Sian, who's a year older than me. We were both jumping on the sofa in the front room of our terraced house on Winchester Road in Redcar, mucking about as we did a lot, when Mam wasn't watching us. Sian was practising her gymnastics and she accidentally swallowed a coin, then tried to grab me when she realised what she'd done. The result was I crashed face first into our glass coffee table. The corner of it went directly into the top part of my eye, hitting some of the nerves in the back of my eye and ripping the skin above it.

I don't remember a thing as I was only two years old, but I know from my mum I was rushed to hospital with blood pouring out of my eye socket and everyone panicking that I might have done serious damage to my sight. The doctors did a good job of fixing me up and my vision was unharmed, but I was left with a big scar and a noticeably lazy right eye. It's possible I'd been born with the turn in my eye and it had just not been detected before the accident, but now it was diagnosed and suddenly it was very obvious. Overnight it became one of my defining characteristics. I had to wear thick glasses, but that was not the worst of it.

I think this could have been the start of me becoming somebody who was nervous and a bit afraid. Mam says I was still the little boy I always was: happy-go-lucky with loads of energy. Too much energy, actually. I had a crazy amount of energy, to the point where I was hyperactive all the time. From as far back as I or anybody else can remember, I never stopped jumping on things, climbing all over the place and kicking a football around. In hindsight, I'm sure there's an argument I should have been tested for ADHD or something similar, though I never was.

By the time I started primary school I was totally obsessed with Middlesbrough FC and I had a blue-and-black plastic toy guitar I always played with, non-stop, like my life depended on it. I loved *SuperTed*, *Captain Bucky O'Hare* and *Thunderbirds* on TV, though I could never sit still through a whole show because I was just so hyper. Mam would constantly be telling me to calm down and sit down, and she became stricter with me after I damaged my eye, because she didn't want me to hurt myself again.

'Don't misbehave! Stop it, James! Calm down! Can't you sit still?'

I sometimes felt like they were the only words she could say to me because she said them so many times. I felt like a nuisance to my mum, in fact. That's my abiding memory: feeling like I was in the way and nothing but trouble. I was always afraid of defying my mum and getting on the wrong side of her. I didn't want her to shout at me, and I was very fearful of doing any more damage to myself. Neither did I want to stand out and give the kids at school more reason to pick on me, but I couldn't stop being hyperactive. I still never stopped tearing around the place, because I physically couldn't, but now I never stopped worrying either.

Sometimes when Mam told me off I got angry, because I wasn't deliberately misbehaving. It was just the way I was.

'It's not fair!' I'd cry. 'You're horrible. I'm not doing anything wrong!'

'You're just like your dad,' Mam would say, and even at a very young age I understood that this was a criticism. She said it with venom. She spat the words.

I couldn't understand this at all, because I thought my dad was cool. I didn't see a great deal of him – he and Mam split up when I was just a year old – but I did still see him. In my earliest memories, Dad lived in a flat nearby and I can remember him picking Sian and me up in his car and taking us there.

I liked to see Dad, even though Mam always kicked off whenever he was even mentioned, shouting and screaming about how he'd let her down, leaving her with two little kids, and what a horrible person he was. She never said this to his face because she refused to speak to him, so me and Sian had to listen to it all, which always upset us and spoilt the visit before it even started. Sometimes Mam changed her mind and didn't let us go with Dad after all. Then he lost his temper and shouted too, and the whole day was ruined.

Dad always did his best with us. He was a nice, placid guy, a good guy: raised in Glasgow, Rangers-mad, enjoyed a beer with the lads, worked locally, looking after rental properties in the town. There was nothing complicated about Dad, and I knew he loved Sian and me. That was all that mattered, so when my mam berated him and made out he was some sort of bad person it confused me. The only time I ever saw him shout was when she provoked him and, if anything, he was the opposite of the angry person she made him out to be.

*Why are you telling me this, Mam? Why are you accusing me of being just like my dad, like he's some kind of monster?*

I couldn't understand it at all. It was impossible to get my head around. I'd listen to what Mam said and try to make sense of it, but I never could. I had no idea why I was being criticised and told off for being like my dad, because what was wrong with him? And why did Mam want to compare me to him if she hated him so much? I was her son and she got super-stressed about me hurting myself physically. Wasn't she bothered about hurting my feelings? Did she *want* to hurt my feelings?

I became a bit paranoid, trying to work all this out, and that's why I think my mental health struggles may have started to take root after I damaged my eye. There had to be something wrong with me, didn't there? Mam was stricter and shouting at me more. She was saying I was like my dad, and that was bad, though I didn't understand why. And the turn in my eye was a very visible sign that there really *was* something wrong with me; I stood out, and the kids at school could see I wasn't like them.

I had to stay out of trouble. I didn't want to hurt myself again or give the bullies at school any more ammunition, and most of all I didn't want Mam to shout at me. Dealing with all these thoughts and fears made me fearful and anxious, all of the time.

I couldn't escape the feelings, ever, and I was on hyper-alert as a matter of course. The fear and anxiety were permanently digging inside me, making my heart beat fast and forging tunnels in my brain that sent my thoughts along routes I don't think they were meant to follow, creating moods I didn't want to feel.

Fear and anxiety. They are feelings that have followed me around my whole life.

# CHAPTER TWO

*What are you afraid of? You know you can sing. Why are you so scared?*

I was standing in the queue for *The X Factor* auditions in Middlesbrough in May 2012, and I was alone with my acoustic guitar. Naturally, I was feeling nervous and afraid.

'No, it's not for me. That's not my journey, Mam.'

That's what I'd said to my mum when she first told me *The X Factor* had a mobile van in town, and that I should get myself down there for an audition.

I didn't want to do it. I was twenty-four years old and had

played in a succession of indie bands for the past eight years. I'd had quite a lot of success locally and had always strongly believed I had enough talent to get a recording contract under my own steam. I had one blow after another though, and the last one had knocked me into a deep depression. For the first time ever I was starting to think it was never going to happen for me and I might as well give up. I couldn't bear the thought, and I didn't want to admit I might need the help of something like *The X Factor*. It didn't feel right for me, and what if I failed to get through? I wouldn't be able to deal with it; I'd never recover.

I tried to fob my mum off by saying my music wasn't mainstream enough, and nor was I. To be fair, I genuinely didn't think an outcast like me would fit into something like *The X Factor*. My lifestyle was not conventional in any way, and hadn't been for a long time. I had demons and drugs in my life; hardly the stuff you would want to lay bare on primetime TV. Mam knew all about this, or at least most of it. She got what I was saying, but still she was having none of it. She had always been my biggest fan when it came to my music. She was convinced that all that mattered was my voice, and she wasn't giving up.

A few days before the auditions I ran out of money and had no electricity in my tiny little council bedsit.

'Mam, lend us a fiver will ya? If ya don't I'll be in the dark for the next few days.'

Mam was always my last resort, after I'd failed to borrow money from any of my mates. The electricity in my bedsit, on the seafront in Saltburn, North Yorkshire, ran from a meter that was fed with £5 cards I had to buy from the local Spar. My friends refused to lend me the money because they knew that I'd probably go and spend it on a bag of weed instead of an electricity card. I'd done that countless times before. I'd look at the fiver in my hand and weigh up what was more important – the weed or the leccy. The weed invariably won, and my mum wasn't daft.

'I tell you what, darlin'. I'll do better than that. I'll give you your train fare to Middlesbrough if you go and audition, and if you do that I'll give you the electricity money too.'

'No, forget it. I don't fit the criteria.'

'But James, you are a phenomenal singer. Your voice is all anyone will be interested in. You've always been destined to be a star! Believe me. Just do it. What have you got to lose?'

'Nah. I'm not the full package, am I? I don't look like a pop star. They won't want me.'

If I'm honest, I was coming out with any excuse I could think of. I genuinely didn't think it was the way for me to go, but in the end I relented. I'm not sure how or why, because I was in a very dark place in my head. I guess I had nothing in the world to lose, and Mam's unshakable belief in me was hard to dismiss.

Ever since I was a small boy she'd told me my voice was amazing and that I had an incredible singing career ahead of me. Having her approval meant so much. Deep down, it was all I ever really wanted, and whenever Mam praised me it lifted my self-esteem and gave me a glimmer of hope that life wasn't so bad after all. Perhaps I wasn't such an outcast and a loser, and maybe my dreams would come true.

'Just do it, James. You're an amazing singer. Do it. Go on.'

Hearing my mam repeat the mantra I'd heard so many times growing up must have been what finally made me agree to go to the *X Factor* audition. It was that word 'amazing'. To hear my mam describe me that way meant so much. She didn't dish out compliments to me she didn't mean, and false praise was certainly not Mam's thing. I'd been a source of worry to her for years, a complete pain in the arse. She wasn't in the business of pandering to me, no way. I knew she really did believe in me. Even though I was now a grown man, her words still had the same magical effect they had on me as a boy.

I took Mam's tenner and got the train to Middlesbrough on my own, because that was my life then. I was a lone wolf, and I stood at the back of the queue outside the mobile *X Factor* van, behind a couple of hundred other hopefuls, not talking to anyone. This was one of the very early auditions, a precursor to the televised ones in the big cities, so it wasn't a massive event. Even so I was as nervous as hell, and I clung onto my acoustic guitar like a crutch.

*What are you afraid of? You know you can sing. Why are you so scared?*

What daunted me the most was the ordeal of auditioning in front of a panel. I'd sung hundreds of times to packed pubs and, with my most recent band – Save Arcade – I'd performed to more than 1,200 people at a local festival. But this was different. I would have to stand directly in front of strangers who were scrutinising me and judging me, not drinking a pint and talking to their mates. I would have to look these people in the eye, and I didn't want to do that. It was hardwired into my brain not to hold eye contact for more than a few seconds, in case anyone spotted my lazy eye and realised how ugly I was.

I tried to calm myself down as I thought about all this and fretted. I reasoned that I hadn't yet seen anyone leave the *X Factor* truck with a smile on their face and waving the slip that meant they were invited back. Somebody had to get through, and I started to think that maybe I could be the best of this bunch. Thanks to my mum I had a huge amount of confidence in my singing ability, but what about my looks? How was I going to cope with being examined at close quarters? What if the people judging me thought I was looking the wrong way, because of my eye?

*What are you looking at, weirdo?*

I heard the school bully in my head and I shrank back to being a small, insecure little boy again, worried to death about whether it looked like I was focusing my eyes the wrong way, and how strange I was and how I didn't fit in and never would. This flash of paranoia was something that happened all the time, usually when I was already feeling fearful and anxious and was at my most vulnerable, as I was now.

I couldn't do it. I couldn't hold anyone's gaze for more than a second or two. I never had, throughout my whole life, so what was I doing here, putting myself through this ordeal, trying to get myself on national television, where every flaw would be picked over?

I left the queue and went to get a coffee. I needed a shot of energy after standing around for ages, and I needed to wake myself up, because I'd barely slept the night before. I'd been up for hour after hour, smoking weed and writing songs about anything that made me feel connected to the world. It's what I did every night. I was on the dole, living on welfare in my scruffy little bedsit that was barely the size of a bathroom, and I was depressed and directionless.

I'd usually sleep for most of the day, and as well as constantly self-medicating with weed I was taking the antidepressant Sertraline, prescribed by my doctor. I was embarrassed to be on those pills. Antidepressants. Just the word made me feel depressed. Back then I thought it held a stigma; it told the world I was a loser, someone who needed a prop. I still took the tablets though, because the combination of weed and prescription drugs seemed to get me by. It was like I'd concocted my own winning formula. The pills suppressed my depressed feelings and the weed pulled me up a bit and made me feel less zombified than I would on the pills alone. That was my theory, my excuse.

I walked back to the queue outside the mobile van. I'd lost my place and thought about getting the train back to Redcar. My bedsit was only three or four stops down the train tracks. I could be back there very soon, smoking a joint and blowing the sharp edges off my anxiety. I could tell Mam I'd auditioned and not got through.

Or I could get back in the queue and keep myself going by telling myself how cool it would be to get through, and how much more I would enjoy sparking up a joint when I got home later, if I'd done well. Maybe it would be worth waiting in this queue. I could achieve something today. I could earn my joint and really savour it.

I chose the latter; fuck knows how, given the sleep-deprived, medicated state I was in. Then suddenly I was in front of a producer called Emma and a cameraman, telling them my genre was acoustic guitar, rap and singing.

I performed a song I'd written called 'Habit', about someone going crazy. The lyrics were about my self-medicating, and how I needed to stop taking my frustrations out on people I love. During my performance, I had no idea if the producer or anybody else liked it, because I didn't look at anyone, and we were in a dark tent at the back of the truck. Afterwards I glanced up and saw Emma grinning like the Cheshire Cat. The cameraman was smiling too, and so were the couple of other people in the tent.

I was asked to perform a cover, and I did Alicia Keys' 'Fallin''.

'We really want to see you again,' Emma said, still grinning.

I was given a slip – one of only three I'd seen handed out all day – and told they wanted me to come to another audition a week or so later, this time in Liverpool.

'Thank you,' I muttered and headed back to the station.

I got on the train and all I could think about was my reward: sparking up that joint. I didn't have the shot of excitement or happiness you might expect after doing well, because the combination of weed and antidepressants suppressed my feelings so much. My emotions were permanently numbed, suspended in a stale middle ground. There were no giddy highs or crashing lows. I was avoiding the depression as best I could, but the price I paid was to function within this narrow, drug-defined margin. At least I was functioning, because that was better than sinking, but I'd forgotten what it was like to feel happy and excited as part of my normal, everyday life. The only time I felt any kind of happiness at all was when I was singing and playing my guitar. The rest of the time I was dead behind the eyes.

I'd been going out with a girl called Lucy for almost two years, and her dad offered to drive me to the audition in Liverpool. I spent the night before smoking loads of weed, as usual, and Lucy and my mum had to phone me repeatedly to nag me to get up, get myself together and get in the car.

When I arrived at the audition I was expecting to see hundreds of people, but there were just fifteen others.

'What do you do this for?' a woman with ginger hair asked me.

She looked sceptical, and I got the impression she'd heard a few generic answers that day and was expecting to hear bullshit.

'To be honest, music's the only thing that make me feel normal. I'm all over the place the rest of the time. I'm detached from reality. Music is what makes me happy and I love doing it.'

The woman was nodding as I spoke and she started smiling from ear to ear.

'I'm really happy to hear that,' she said.

I sang my own take on Lauryn Hill's version of Frankie Valli's 'Can't Take My Eyes Off Of You', with a rap in the second verse.

Now everyone in the room was smiling and nodding, and then they asked me more questions, to which I gave straight and honest answers. I told them I was unemployed and gave a bit of information about my background, and I said that, yes, I could come to the next auditions in Newcastle. It was explained to me that these were the ones at which Dermot O'Leary would come out into the crowd and do interviews, and I realised then that this Liverpool stage was used to select candidates who Dermot could potentially chat to, and might ultimately be featured on the audition show.

I started to feel I'd done something cool, and I was feeling better about myself than I had in a long time. Lucy came from a lovely, supportive family, and her parents both had very good jobs. I felt this was my chance to finally gain a bit of respect and show them, and everybody else, that I wasn't the waste of space I had been for so many years.

*Don't get carried away. You know you don't fit the criteria. It will probably all come to nothing. You'll be spat out of this machine. You'll feel like shit. What the hell are you putting yourself through this for?*

The chatter in my brain did its very best to drag me down. Anyone who has suffered from depression will understand this. It's like having your worst enemy living inside your head, instantly pouring cold water on any remotely positive thoughts you have. I'd try to argue with the demons who did that. I'd try to tell myself I did stand a chance, but I was weak by comparison, and the negative chatter always scored more points.

I decided almost straight away that I needed to come off the weed, to give myself the best chance of doing well in Newcastle. The audition was six weeks away, so I had time. I started to think about coming off the antidepressants too, because I was worried the tablets made me look messed up. I was having a lot of paranoid thoughts about being in front of a camera and looking like I was high, or gurning like a crazy person.

*What if the tablets make me worse, when I come off the weed? What if I feel weird and numb and can't perform? What if I look like a zombie?*

I'd never taken antidepressants on their own before, without the weed, and I began to panic about what would happen. I was in real conflict with myself for days, and I wanted to make it stop. I wasn't used to having the sort of pressure in my life that the impending *X Factor* audition was putting me under. I didn't have a job or any proper responsibilities, and I had no idea how to cope with the stress of this competition. It was so hard to deal with. Half of me wanted to run away and forget I'd ever embarked on this journey, and the other half of me knew this was the best chance I'd ever had to show everybody I cared about what I could do.

Normally, I had nothing good to tell my family, ever. I was the black sheep. The awkward, wayward son with anger issues. The brother who caused nothing but hassle and heartache for all his pretty sisters.

I wanted everyone I loved to see I was better than that. I wanted to prove myself to my mum and dad and all my siblings, and to Lucy and her parents. Most of all, I needed to take this opportunity for myself, because the hard truth was I might not get a record deal any other way, and making music was my only ambition in life. There was no plan B, not ever.

Overnight I stopped smoking weed and I came off the pills. It seemed like a good idea at the time.

# CHAPTER THREE

*Don't step on the cracks. Stay on the*
*paving stones. Avoid the spaces in between*

I was walking home from primary school and concentrating hard on where I put my feet.

I was convinced that if I stood on the cracks in between the paving stones then my mum would be in a bad mood when I got home from school, and I didn't want her to be in a bad mood: this was always the very last thing I wanted.

*Don't step on the cracks. Stay on the paving stones. Avoid the spaces in between.*

When she was in a good mood, my mum was the most amazing person in the world to be around. She was so vivacious and full of life, and she made everyone around her feel positive and passionate about whatever she was doing or talking about.

'I absolutely love this track!' she'd say, playing tapes and turning up the stereo in the kitchen as she cooked Smiley Faces, fish fingers or beans for tea.

She danced around, full of energy, as she sang along to all the greats like Prince, Marvin Gaye, Michael Jackson, David Bowie and George Michael, encouraging me to sing too. The first album I ever bought was *Waking Up the Neighbours* by Bryan Adams. I'd play my favourite track, 'Thought I'd Died and Gone to Heaven', and Mam would sing along with me. We'd both be buzzing, feeling as thick as thieves as we indulged our shared passion together.

Mam has got a beautiful voice and I loved to hear her sing. She was so full of life and positivity whenever she was singing, and I'd forget all about the bad stuff we went through. *This* was the Mam I loved. Her emotions were extreme, always at one end of the scale or the other, so when she was in a good mood she'd be on a real high. When she was like this I'd look at her and think, 'You're the best person in the world. You are *amazing*!' I couldn't imagine being around anyone better than my mam.

'Wow, your voice is *amazing*,' she'd say to me whenever I joined in. 'It's phenomenal! You have a really beautiful voice, James.'

She shone with pride and enthusiasm as she told me I was the best, time and time again. She was so encouraging that she made me really believe in myself, one hundred per cent. Her compliments filled me with so much confidence about my musical talent. Mam made me feel I was a really great singer. I was going to make phenomenal music and be a big star. This wasn't false praise. She truly believed that, and she made me believe it too.

I absolutely loved my mum when she was in this mood. To receive such high praise from her was so precious to me. I craved her love and attention and held it close. It meant so much. My mum – or at least this version of my mum – was my best friend in the whole world.

Unfortunately, she wasn't always like that. I didn't have the words to define or explain it at the time, but I know now that Mam suffered from BPD (Borderline Personality Disorder). As a result, she had extreme mood swings, and I mean *extreme*. When she was in a bad mood she was vile and vicious, and my best friend became my worst enemy. Mam was a person who could stab me in the back at any time, and because of how her illness made her behave, I grew to be afraid of her, all the time, because I didn't know which version I was going to get.

*Don't step on the cracks. Stay on the paving stones. Avoid the spaces in between. If you step on the cracks, Mam will be in a bad mood.*

My real mum is wonderful, warm and caring. My real mum is vivacious, positive and absolutely amazing. It is thanks to her that I have the career and life I have today. She gave me the most incredible confidence in my musical ability and, as I've said, I would not have even gone to audition for *The X Factor* without her.

My 'other mum' – the version of my mum who was ruled by extreme depressive moods beyond her control – was the polar opposite. Now I understand the illness and the damage it can do to a person's life and personality, I don't blame her for how she behaved during my childhood, but I can't forget, because her illness has had a huge and very damaging effect on my life.

'Where's my season ticket?' I asked Mam one night after I got home from primary school. 'There's a game tomorrow and it's not in the drawer.'

I hadn't stepped on the spaces in between the paving stones, but even so Mam was in a bad mood. I could tell the moment I got in the door. She wasn't dancing or singing, there was tension in the air and her face was expressionless as she looked at me.

'It's gone, sorry,' Mam replied coldly.

My heart sank and my throat tightened. I was eight years old and totally obsessed with Middlesbrough FC. I'd been so excited about the game, but Mam's mood had changed mine in a flash. I was instantly on high alert and I could feel the panic rising. Mam was clearly in one of her black moods and this was not going to end well. It never did.

My stepdad, a lovely guy called Ronnie Rafferty, knew how mad I was about Middlesbrough and his friend had managed to get me a season ticket, which was my most prized possession.

Mam had met Ronnie when I was three, after being on her own with Sian and me for a couple of years, following the split from my dad. I really liked Ronnie and couldn't remember a time when he was not around. It was typical of him to have sorted out the season ticket for me: in Ronnie, I felt I had an ally. From a very early age I felt he understood that Mam didn't always treat me fairly. Maybe he had already worked out something that I did later, which was that I reckoned Mam saw herself in my big sister Sian. They were girls together, whereas I was the odd one out, the ugly-looking boy, the one who reminded her of the ex-husband she hated with a passion.

Mam met Dad when she was a bubbly, happy-go-lucky sixteen-year-old and he was twenty-six and working as a local DJ. Dad had been married twice before and already had my brother, Neil, who's ten years older than me. My mum and dad were together for five years before they married, and they divorced two years later, amid accusations of lies and cheating on both sides. Mam was just twenty-three when she found herself on her own with two kids. She would have deleted my dad from her life if she could have, but of course they had me and Sian, aged just one and two. Dad always fought to see us, so she was stuck with him in her life.

Meeting and marrying a great guy like Ronnie didn't appear to make any difference to how Mam viewed my dad. The wounds she'd been left with never seemed to heal one bit; instead they dripped poison throughout my childhood.

Ronnie and Mam had my little sister Jasmin when I was seven years old. Dad had remarried too by this time, and he and his new wife Jackie had my other sister Charlotte the same year. I was besotted with both my little sisters and Mam and Ronnie were madly in love, but even so my mum seemed obsessed with holding on to the traumas of the past. Her view of Dad never, ever changed. She hated him so much, and when she was in a bad mood, she hated me.

'What d'you mean, it's gone? How can my season ticket be gone, Mam? It was in the drawer, where I always keep it.'

Mam told me flatly that she'd had a phone call from the school, telling her I'd been misbehaving. This was a common occurrence because I did behave like a little shit at school. I never did anything really bad, but I did like to play the class clown, and I was always that kid making faces through the window if I got thrown out of class, or putting all my energy into coming out with the line that would make all the other kids laugh and disrupt the lesson.

I can see now that I behaved like that because I didn't get the attention I wanted at home. If I tried to put a point across to Mam it seemed like I always got interrupted or told to shut up. I'm sure that's why I became completely obsessed with things, like football or playing with my toy guitar incessantly. I needed to latch on to something, to feel I had a purpose and that something really mattered to me.

Anyhow, Mam got phone calls all the time from the school and didn't usually take them very seriously, but this time she chose to have a go at me, in a way she knew would really get to me.

'Like I said, it's gone.'

'What d'you *mean* it's gone?'

My heart was drumming wildly but Mam looked calm and seemed completely unmoved.

'Where the hell is my season ticket? It was in that drawer last night, I know it was. What have you done with it, Mam?'

I was starting to properly panic now, thinking I was going to miss the game, but still Mam didn't appear to care one bit.

'It's just gone, sorry,' she repeated in an icy voice, and I could tell that she was deliberately trying to wind me up, as she often did when the mood took her.

'Give me the ticket!' I raged. 'The Boro are playing tomorrow. I need my season ticket, Mam!'

I was so angry, and I was shouting at the top of my voice and stomping around, fists balled, full of fury.

'Look at you! Why are you shouting? What did I tell you? You're just like your dad!'

'I hate you! Just give me my ticket, Mam!'

'Get outside, James, NOW!'

Mam was staring at me with eyes of steel. She opened the back door and kicked me outside in the cold afternoon drizzle. She'd done this so many times and I couldn't believe this was happening again. I stood in the back yard, trying to make some sense of this, with so many questions going around in my head that I thought I was losing my mind.

*Why is she doing this? Why is Mam treating me like this? She doesn't usually go off like this when the school phones up complaining about me. Why today? Why is it always me she picks on? What is wrong with me?*

I wanted to get back inside and so I threw something at the house to get Mam's attention. I didn't mean to cause any damage, but whatever I threw smashed the window on the back door. Now Mam really did have a reason to have a go at me.

'I wish I'd never had you!' she screeched, flinging the door open like a demon. 'I wish I'd had an abortion.'

I was so confused by that.

'What do you mean? Do you mean you wish I wasn't . . . here?'

'Yes!' she spat. 'I wish so badly I'd never had *you*.'

She said it with such venom and so sincerely it killed me. I felt so worthless. My life was so insignificant and disposable.

*My mam thinks I'm a piece of shit.*

I stood in the corner and cried and screamed.

'Bitch!' I sobbed. 'I hate you!'

I complained to my dad the next time I saw him, like I often did.

'It's just your mam, son. It's just how she is.'

*Brilliant.*

I think Sian could see the injustice of how I was treated, but she didn't want to get on the wrong side of Mam. She was only a year older than me, after all, and she was afraid of Mam in these moods too. Sian's way of dealing with the situation was always to avoid confrontation and do whatever she could to keep the peace, even if it meant siding with Mam when deep down she didn't want to. The result was I always felt very alone in the house.

I got sent to bed early after I smashed the window. There were plenty of nights when I cried into my pillow, and on this particular night, still without my season ticket and with Mam's cruel words kicking at my brain, I really lost it. I was full of confusion and so much anger and rage. I felt utterly dejected and I screamed into my pillow. It was like a primal scream that I couldn't control, because I was so deliriously upset.

*What am I here for if my own mam doesn't want me here? What is the point of life? What is it for? Why are we here if we don't even love each other?*

I thought about images I saw on TV or on posters and in adverts, of mothers and sons and happy families. That was what it was supposed to be like. A mother's love for her son was meant to be unconditional, yet my experience wasn't like that at all. My version of that story was the most black and horrible one imaginable.

I lay in the darkness and I couldn't figure out why my life was like this. I was a bit loud at times, a bit hyper and a bit weird. I definitely felt weird, in a misfit kind of way, but was that what I'd done wrong, just being a bit loud and hyper and weird?

The same thoughts went around and around in my head,

and I drove myself mad trying to work out what was so wrong with me to make my mum hate me so much.

*Does she think I'm too ugly? Is it because my sisters are pretty and I'm a little jam-jar-glasses-wearing kid with a turned-in eye? Am I the black sheep of the family? Is this the way it will always be? I'm a piece of shit, and it's never going to change. I guess I might as well just play the part.*

I wanted to sleep, to push all these thoughts out. When I shut my eyes, I saw piles and piles of paper. Great slabs of it. Underneath the huge piles was a tiny little toothpick, being crushed by the weight of all the paper. I could feel the pressure. The flimsy little thing was going to break under all the pressure.

I had this vision many times during my childhood, sometimes in different forms. On other nights, the paper was replaced with big slabs of meat, bearing down on a pin or a matchstick that was bending or snapping under the weight.

There was another vision too. There were loads of times when I lay in bed and saw images of two people screaming at each other. It was really odd. I had fuzzy flashes in my eyes – the sort of dazzling starbursts you get if you put pressure on your eyes and then let go. The two screaming people were always inside the flashes, shouting in each other's faces, and sometimes the faces came out of my bedroom walls.

'Ronnie! I'm seeing that thing again!'

My stepdad would come and try to calm me down whenever I shouted for him, but I never felt calm. The anxiety I felt as a child became more prevalent and more debilitating. When I look back it feels like I spent most of my time in that state when I was growing up, feeling desperately upset, sobbing into my pillow and struggling with the fact that I felt under pressure and had no control over my situation.

# CHAPTER FOUR

*Get your breath. Don't keel over. Don't pass out.*

'I want you both to be there. You don't have to talk to each other, but I can't deal with you arguing or shouting. This is too big a deal for me and I'm nervous enough as it is. Can you just come down for the day and support me, with no drama?'

'James, it'll be an absolute honour to be there,' Mam said. She was buzzing about me being invited to the televised interviews in Newcastle. This was exactly what she'd hoped would happen when she twisted my arm to go to the initial audition on the mobile truck in Middlesbrough, and she was already convinced I had what it took to win *The X Factor*. 'I'll do whatever it takes, darlin', you know I will. This is your big chance.'

Dad agreed too, even though he hates being in the spotlight and the idea he might be filmed with me really did not appeal to him.

'If that's what you want, son, I'll do it. I know what this means to you.'

I'd thought long and hard about inviting them both along. I needed all the support I could get and wanted them there, but my nerves were already wild and I knew I could not deal with any added stress. That is why I had to lay it on the line for them the way I did. I was grateful when they agreed to come and to put their differences to one side, at least for a day, and as the audition approached I even started to believe it could be a beautiful thing, getting the family together again on such a big day for me. Whatever had gone on in the past, I knew my parents loved me and wanted me to sort my life out. Maybe this would bring a bit of peace and harmony to the family after all this time.

*Do they just feel sorry for me? Will Mam argue with Dad and ruin everything? Things always fall through. Oh my God, what have I done?*

For once my internal worries were not crazy or irrational. My parents had let me down in the past, when I was at a crucial crossroads in my life and most needed them to be there for me. It was too late now though. I had to keep the faith and believe this was for the best.

The night before the audition I slept on the sofa at my best mate Michael Dawson's house in Middlesbrough. Our other mate Paul was there, because he was driving me to Newcastle, and we'd stayed up talking until 6 a.m. as Paul had a few things going on.

*Shit. I've only had an hour and a half's sleep. It doesn't matter. I won't get through anyhow. It'll just be another knock-back. I'll end up going back to my bedsit and my stoner lifestyle.*

I put a packet of antidepressants in my pocket before we left the house. I'd managed to go without, since binning them after the Liverpool audition, but it hadn't been easy at all. I got rid of them because I was paranoid about looking zombified on stage, but now I was super-nervous about going to pieces in front of the judges, because without the pills I was feeling my anxiety much more intensely than I normally did. Just having the pills in my pocket helped. If the nerves got too bad, at least I had something to reach for, something that would deaden my emotions and suppress my fears.

It wasn't just my mam and dad who were supporting me. When I got to Newcastle all my close family was there, as well as some of my closest friends. It was overwhelming to see everyone together, but I was too anxious to enjoy the occasion. I can remember making conversation but not really being there in my head, because all I could think about was how scared I felt, and how the hell I was going to get through this day.

*Oh fuck, it's Dermot O'Leary and he's about to talk to me.*

I was star-struck by Dermot and I immediately started to panic, thinking I had nothing to tell him. He was so full of life and I had to give him something.

Mam stepped in and told Dermot who she was, describing herself as a 'very proud mum', and Dad shyly introduced himself too. Just having my mam and dad standing either side of me was overwhelming, let alone anything else. We probably looked like one big close-knit, happy family.

*Wild*.

When Dermot spoke to me I explained how everyone had pulled together for me that day, and then I was taken aside to give an interview. I hadn't prepared what I was going to say at all. The sun was dazzling and I was blinking and squinting as I started to answer questions from a producer.

'My mam and dad split up when I was really young,' I said, with the camera rolling.

I had to say something and I wanted to be honest and not sugar-coat my life.

'The difficult thing for me was that my mam and dad didn't have any sort of relationship for my entire life. I went off the rails, especially at school. I used to get suspended, thrown out. I ended up sleeping rough sometimes, so I volunteered myself into foster care. I didn't want to be involved in any of the arguing any more. I just wanted to get away. Initially music was a coping mechanism. Today is the first time my mam and dad have been together in twenty-two years.'

I could see the producers' eyes light up when I mentioned foster care, but the only reason I said it was because that was my life and I wanted to be truthful. Mam was interviewed next and she got very emotional, saying she questioned whether she'd done enough for me in the past, and explaining how moved she was when she heard me express my worries and anxieties through my music.

We had to wait around for six or seven hours that day, and my nerves were getting progressively worse. Eventually we were moved to a pen and I started pacing up and down like a caged animal, with my heart beating and my breathing getting shallower and more laboured. All the while I had one hand in my pocket, wondering whether to take a pill. At one point I was asked to step into the office to have a chat about my welfare.

'Are you all right? You look like you're having a nervous breakdown.'

'I'm just super-nervous. I'll be fine, thanks.'

*I'm not fine at all. I'm losing my mind. I'm going to have to take one of these pills in my pocket or I won't be able to do this. The nerves are just too crazy.*

I swallowed a pill an hour before I was due on stage and it settled me down almost instantly. I started to breathe better but I also became a little bit blank and had nothing to say, so I started a whole new round of worry about whether I'd be able to speak properly to the judges.

Then there I was, under the hot lights, trying to look confident as I walked onto the stage. It was too surreal. I was standing in front of Gary Barlow, Nicole Scherzinger, Tulisa and Louis Walsh, telling them who I was and what I was going to perform. I didn't want to look any of them in the eye, and amid all of this fear I suddenly heard myself asking them if it was OK if I used my acoustic guitar.

*Why did you say that? Of course you can use your guitar. I just want to sing now. Get your breath. Don't keel over. Don't pass out.*

Gary was a god to me. As a singer-songwriter he'd had the sort of phenomenal success I wanted to emulate. Not only had he written multiple hit songs, he was such a cool guy. In my mind, he was the one who could best judge me, and I thought that if I put myself in his shoes I'd be super-critical of me. The idea he might reject me – or that any of the judges might publicly reject me – was utterly terrifying.

I chose to perform an acoustic version of Tulisa's 'Young', which was number one at the time. I thought it was a good tactic to pick one of the judges' own songs, and I reckoned that if I could make a pop dance song by a female my own, it would show ultimate artistry.

Now I was there, I wasn't so sure. I was going to rap in a northern accent. I was going to sing from my throat and gut. I didn't look like Justin Bieber or any other 'proper' pop star. This was all too scary, too big a gamble. I wanted to turn and run away and keep going until I was back in my flat and could light a joint and . . .

I heard my cue, and now I was performing the song, putting my all into it and instantly feeling better than I had all day, because at last I had escaped into my music. When I looked up at the end I saw all four judges get to their feet and give me a standing ovation, and the audience was going absolutely crazy.

*This is freaky. I feel so embarrassed. Just chill. Try to look confident.*

'Best audition of the day.'

*Tulisa! She looks gorgeous. She likes it, and it's her song! Thank you. Say it out loud. Say thank you. Stay calm. Don't mess up now. Gary's going next.*

'OK, James. We sit here all day and we watch lots and lots of people stand on this stage. Ninety-nine per cent of people, I sit there and go, OK we need to change this, they need to do that, we need to try this, but if anyone dares touch what you do . . .'

People were screaming and cheering and my heart was trying to break out of my chest. I was working so hard just to stay upright and appear normal that I ended up looking completely underwhelmed.

'Because what you do is so good . . . you should be very proud. That was a fantastic audition. Well done!'

Louis had his say and told me I was a 'real original' and had a future in the industry. If I'm honest it sounded like a ready-made comment he'd used before, but at least it was positive. Three down and one to go: Nicole.

I thought Nicole was the most beautiful woman in the world. I'd fancied her when she was in the Pussycat Dolls, and now she was smiling straight at me, her eyes shining as she explained to me that I was the reason she came on the show, because she was looking for an artist to inspire her. 'That's exactly what you did today. You inspired me, because you sat on that stage and you bared your soul to us.'

I got four yeses and my pass to boot camp. It was the best result I could have hoped for, but I had to force myself to smile. I didn't want to show my teeth because they were so crooked. I would take the mickey out of myself and say they looked like a burnt fence, but it was no joke; my teeth contributed to my feelings of paranoia and freakishness. Even before I got off the stage I could feel the pressure weighing down on me, and as I said thank you and walked away the chatter was already raging in my head.

*This could all go wrong. Something is going to happen. You don't look the part. What the hell have you started this for? Fuck. There's no going back.*

Dermot appeared and I realised this was the bit where I was meant to provide a soundbite, but I didn't want to come out with a cheesy line. I stayed calm and said the bare minimum – something bland and deadpan about feeling overwhelmed, and how I just couldn't describe how good it felt.

Right from the start I knew, subconsciously at least, that I only stood a chance in the competition if I stayed true to myself and didn't get sucked into trying to conform to something that wasn't me. I was never going to be a shiny-suited pin-up and I was not going to compromise myself by getting pulled into the machine. I wanted a long-term career, not overnight success that might not even last. Ultimately, I wanted the sceptics who didn't even like *The X Factor* to respect me as an artist and to judge me on my music, and for that to happen I knew deep down that I had to stay true to who I was.

Mam was more of a natural for the cameras, giving the producers what they wanted by hugging me and telling me I was amazing and she was so proud. Dad gamely did his bit too, coming in for a group hug and saying I was phenomenal. My parents had done their very best for me that day and I was very thankful to them both, but I can't pretend this felt like a breakthrough in terms of how things would be between the two families in the future. My emotions were subdued. Maybe the numbing effect of the antidepressant pill I'd taken had something to do with it, but the painful truth was, twenty-odd years of pain were not going to be healed in a day, no way. This was a tiny little sticking plaster on a very deep wound and it was unsettling and upsetting to recognise that fact.

Still, I really appreciated everyone around me. My sisters and friends were smiling and crying and all saying the same thing: 'You shocked us! You seemed like you weren't all there beforehand because you were so quiet, and then BAM! You switched it on. Well done! You can win it, James!'

Until now I hadn't dared let myself believe I would go through to the next round, let alone go all the way to the judges' houses or the live shows. Now it was starting to sink in that my audition had changed everything. Only two auditions that day got a standing ovation from the judges. Things had gone really well for me and the negative chatter in my head was finally starting to be drowned out by positive thoughts.

*I don't just want to win. I want to be the best* X Factor *winner of all time. I want to be taken seriously as an artist by people beyond the show, and I want my career to last forever. Maybe I really can do it. This is my chance. It's finally time to turn my life around. I have to up my game.*

# CHAPTER FIVE

*Do other people have conversations in their
head like this, or is it just me who's crazy?*

'We're moving to Bahrain, son.'

'Where's that, Mam?'

'It's in the Middle East. Can you explain it to him,
Ronnie?'

I was nine years old. For as long as I could remember Ronnie
had been training as some kind of computer engineer. Mam
was mostly a stay-at-home mum, although she was very pretty

and did some modelling from time to time, for local magazines and catwalk shows.

We didn't have much money and lived from week to week. I don't remember us ever going without, but if the school brought out a new piece of uniform me and Sian were always the last kids to get it, and only after we'd been told off by the teachers. Mam didn't think that kind of thing was important, and I had the same green coat throughout primary school. I wore it so much I was known as the kid with the green coat, and it doubled as a goalpost so many times that over the years it took on a notoriety of its own and became my trademark.

Our house, on Winchester Road, had two bedrooms and a tiny box room you could only just fit a very small single bed into. We were quite cooped up in there I suppose, especially when my little sister Jasmin came along, but the good thing was that we lived right by a crescent and a bit of green space, where lots of kids played out. We'd vandalise the 'no ball games' sign the council put up and play football regardless: nothing would stop me kicking a ball, and I'd be out of the house at every opportunity.

Our neighbourhood was as rough as any part of Redcar and kids would often fight in our street. Loads of scraps took place on the crescent – it was a prime spot – and I got involved in my fair share of them. I was brave, and if any kids came down the street and nicked our football I'd be the first to confront them. Physical challenges never bothered me: I'd always be the first to check out a haunted shack or stand up to a bully. It was the sneaky sideways glances or the feeling I was being talked about behind my back that rattled me. Survival of the fittest was so much simpler. It was what I was used to and how life was on our street, and I felt at home on Winchester Road.

Being told we were leaving – and going to Bahrain – came as a massive shock. I knew nothing whatsoever about the place and I was immediately on my guard, fretting and worrying and feeling scared to death.

'How far is it to the Middle East and what's it like in Bahrain, Ronnie?' I asked anxiously. I had a hundred questions.

Ronnie said it was about 4,000 miles from Middlesbrough to the Middle East, and he explained it took about ten and a half hours to get there on a plane.

'It's sunny all the time and we'll live in a lovely big house on a compound with a pool. We'll even have a housemaid.'

'A housemaid? Wow.'

What I really wanted to know was how the hell I was going to watch Middlesbrough play.

I respected and admired Ronnie. He'd worked very hard for years and had landed a job as an account manager for a software company based in the Middle East. He'd clearly done really well for himself, and I trusted him. The weather and the lifestyle in Bahrain did sound amazing, but I just couldn't get my head round it.

Life was too confusing to me already, and I just wanted to stay at Winchester Road and play football for as many hours of the day as I could. Also, even though I was only very young, I'd already discovered how fascinating girls were. I fancied a girl called Louise who lived on our road, and I loved seeing her every day. The thought of not seeing her ever again made me want to cry.

My head was full of so many negatives. The idea of leaving my school scared me a lot. I was always grateful to be there, around other kids, and to be busy and occupied and out of the house. I loved the feeling of belonging, being in something together, having fun and just feeling part of whatever was going on at school. I can't say I liked the lessons much, but whatever I had to do to get by in the classroom was worth it, because being in school was so much better than being on hyper-alert at home, anxious about my mum's moods and not having any control over what might happen next.

'Wake up, James!' my teacher said, so many times.

I tended to switch off and daydream, and those words always made me feel paranoid. In fact, whenever anybody said anything remotely negative to me at school I'd go into my shell; either that or I'd get angry.

Every time the teacher told me to wake up I was worried she could tell I was not like everybody else, and that I lived in another world, in my head. There was so much noise and chat going on in my brain all the time as I tried to understand the confusing things that happened in my life. With Bahrain thrown into the mix, the clatter was louder and more alarming than ever.

One of the many things that baffled me was that I was always popular with the girls at school. I had curtains, not a cool haircut like most of the other boys, and I knew I was ugly because of the jam-jar glasses I had to wear to correct the turn in my eye and my short-sighted vision. Even though I was confused by the girls' reaction to me, I was sure of one thing: I always felt good when the girls paid me attention.

Even at this young age I was 'going out' with someone different every week, and I'd flirt with the girls and try different ways of talking to them. Looking back, it was as if I was trying to morph myself into another character because I knew, deep down, I was not like everyone else.

There was one very pretty girl called Sophie who all the boys fancied, and she suddenly took an interest in me. It felt amazing. The only time I got positive attention at home was when I was singing with my mum. When Mam complimented me on my voice it was the most incredible feeling in the world, and I appreciated and enjoyed her praise so much. Maybe that's why I gravitated towards the girls; they might give me compliments too, and I craved that feeling, of being appreciated and admired.

I started going out with Sophie, and for a very short time I thought I couldn't be that disgusting after all. I loved her attention, but the only problem was, I was so panicky and scared I dumped her after just one day. My nerves were just wild; I couldn't deal with them and I was terrified that she would dump me, when she found out what an odd kid I really was.

I had a best mate on our street called Dean, who was the only mixed-race child in the neighbourhood. There was a bunch of kids who picked on him and were always throwing water balloons at him. I didn't know why and couldn't understand it, and I befriended him because I saw that he was a bit different, like me. I'd go to his house and we'd hang out or play football together. If Dean wasn't around I'd often just kick a ball around for hours on my own.

'Goal!' I'd yell, running around celebrating, all by myself. If anyone was watching they'd have thought I was crazy. I'd commentate on my moves, cheer for myself, bring myself on as a substitute in an imaginary Premiership match, the works. I had a whole match playing inside my head, and I'd be on the pitch alongside great Boro players like Juninho and Ravanelli. Sometimes I wondered what people on the street thought of me, and I had conversations about this with myself.

*Do the neighbours think I'm mad? Why am I the only kid out here on my own, doing this? Do other people have conversations in their head like this, or is it just me who's crazy?*

I would never have told anyone what was happening inside my skull. Even though Mam was a very emotional person I wasn't brought up to analyse thoughts and feelings. You spoke when you needed to find your footy boots or to ask what was for tea. Conversations were mostly functional, and because of the way my mum could be I kept the chat to a minimum, so as not to get on her bad side.

'Bahrain will be great, James,' Mam said. 'You'll love it there!'

I really didn't think so, but I didn't argue. Instead I thought again and again about all the things I would miss at home, and how afraid I was. My brain was running wild and second-guessing what this strange place would be like. Sian didn't want to go either, which fuelled my negative reaction.

When I told the kids at school I was moving to the Middle East some of the boys taunted me.

'Ha ha, James is going to live in the desert!'

That shook me. I imagined living in the middle of nowhere, surrounded by nothing but sand and camels. Sian and I were best mates then, and we tried to conjure up images of what it could be like. We heard Mam telling her mates all the time that it would be 'glamorous' and so we imagined exotic scenes, like you'd see in holiday adverts, of palm trees swaying in the breeze, glistening hotels and swimming pools sparkling in the sunshine. I was still scared though, and I feared the worst. We really could be going to live in the middle of a big, empty desert.

I'd barely been outside Boro before, let alone got on a plane and flown thousands of miles away to a foreign country. There were a few times when Dad took Sian and me down the coast to the Primrose Valley Holiday Park in Filey, which was only about an hour and a half away in the car, just past Scarborough. He also took us up to Scotland to visit his side of the family every once in a while.

Dad has a lovely big family up in Glasgow. I loved visiting them. My gran – Dad's mam – was a real sweetheart. She doted on us non-stop, wouldn't stop feeding us and giving us treats, and she would bathe Sian and me in the sink when we were little. Whenever I was around Gran and all my Scottish aunties and uncles and cousins I felt a part of a very warm and loving family culture. It was how I imagined all families should be, wrapped up in a warm bubble of love, pulling together. It was always sad to say goodbye and go back to our reality, with Mam ranting and raving about Dad and our family divided the way it was.

It seemed like we went through exactly the same drama every time Dad collected us and dropped us off, with Mam kicking off before he arrived, but never talking to him because she hated him so much. I'd feel super-anxious with my heart beating out of my chest, wishing all the conflict would stop and feeling scared to say or do anything that might make things worse.

Hearing Mam screaming would remind me of what I saw in my mind's eye when I was alone in my room at night: the starburst flashes with two shouting faces inside them, or the same angry faces coming out of the walls. The bedroom I shared with Sian had a frieze with Disney figures on it. Goofy and Daffy Duck were painted in bright colours, but they would fade into the background or contort into black angry shapes when the shouting faces came out.

When Mam and Dad split up there was a bitter custody battle over Sian and me, because Mam didn't want Dad to see us at all after they got divorced. Dad fought for his rights and won the battle, but the war was never over.

There were other sources of conflict, on top of the ongoing feud between my parents. It was obvious to me that my dad's wife Jackie and my mum didn't like each other at all. It felt at the time like all Sian and I ever heard when we went over to Dad and Jackie's bungalow were comments about Mam and all the things she'd said and done that were wrong. I've always respected Jackie as my dad's wife but I found it hard to fully accept her as part of my family, and I think that is why. I felt she should not get involved at all, and Dad should not join in, as he did sometimes.

Sometimes I'd snap. 'Can you just stop it? Leave Mam alone!'

I'd be accused of being a 'mummy's boy' when I stood up for my mum, and this made me furious. I wanted Dad to take my side, but he naturally shies away from conflicts and he never did. I got that he didn't want to fall out with his wife – he was on his fourth marriage, after all – but it seemed to me like it was anything for an easy life. I was angry with each of them for letting this cycle repeat, over and over again.

*Why can't everyone shut up? Why can't Mam stop shouting? Why can't everyone stop going on about the past? What is the point of all this noise and trouble?*

However bad things got, I desperately wanted to believe that both my parents were good people, and I wanted to feel safe and protected by them, not fearful of what I might hear at Dad's or how loud the shouting would be from Mam. Unfortunately, I could never escape the reality that both my parents had a major issue with each other. And even though they both loved me and didn't set out to mess me up, they did.

Music was my only saving grace, with both my parents. As with my mum, Dad and me never failed to connect when we listened to records. He was, and still is, incredibly passionate about rock music. He'd sit up all night listening to Led Zep, Def Leppard and AC/DC, and he would often explain to me, in painstaking detail, why the music was so beautiful. He inspired me and educated me from a young age, helping me understand and believe in rock music, and I'm very grateful to him for that. Sharing in his passion has certainly influenced my music over the years, and it was another one of the many things I was going to miss about home when we went to Bahrain.

In hindsight, I'm shocked by how much my childhood memories are tainted by the omnipresent threat of Mam slagging Dad off, and of hearing Jackie and sometimes Dad making snide comments and criticising Mam behind her back. Jackie's remarks about my mum were as upsetting as my mum's constant criticisms of Dad. Even if I'd had an argument with Mam and was really pissed off with her, I hated hearing her slagged off, especially by Jackie. The situation was toxic and dysfunctional and I was angry with all three of them, because it was the same every time I saw my dad.

When we packed up our lives and flew to Bahrain I have no recollection of saying goodbye to Dad or making plans to keep in touch, even though we were leaving for good, to all intents and purposes. Dad remembers us both being terribly upset and Mam making no secret of the fact she didn't even want him to phone us up, but I can't remember any feelings or tears. I'm sure I've blocked the sadness out, and I guess this may be because of the tension and trauma that always surrounded any time I spent with my dad.

They say that when a child suffers trauma their nervous system goes into 'fight or flight' mode. I think this happened to me. I've realised there are huge chunks of time in my childhood that I can't remember. I was always on edge, hyper-aware of threats around me. Sometimes I got very angry, super-fast, and I'd argue with Mam and throw things or even break stuff. Other times I went the other way and shut down as a method of protecting myself, because I couldn't cope with the noise and the drama and the fear. In those times of intense anger or shutdown I must have stopped recording memories, because they were too frightening and painful to keep hold of.

I had no idea how I was going to survive in Bahrain. It was a leap into the unknown, and because of the way life had always been for me, I instinctively feared the worst.

# CHAPTER SIX

## *All you have to do is deliver your voice. Get it right. You can do this*

There was about a month between my Newcastle audition and boot camp and it was a gap I could have done without, because I was lost in the space. I tried to do my best to prepare myself mentally but I found each day a struggle and began worrying about every part of my life. I felt super-anxious all the time, worrying not just about my performance but about everybody's issues and all the burdens in my life.

My mum and dad had managed to stay on civil terms after

coming together to support me but I was scared about what might happen next.

*What if I make it through to the live shows? What if Mam and Dad are in the audience together? How will they get on? How will I cope?*

Lucy, my girlfriend, was a few years younger than me and was a very sensitive, emotional person. I'd seen her get incredibly anxious just watching me perform in local 'battle of the bands' competitions, and I started seriously worrying that the X *Factor* process was going to kill her.

*I have to finish with Lucy. She's such a lovely, fragile girl. I'm going to bring her pain and problems. I can't take her with me into this process. It will destroy us both.*

The worries I had about Lucy were so intense they were making me ill. I couldn't sleep properly or think straight because I was fretting all the time about her and our relationship. I was messing about with my antidepressants again too, trying to carry on without them as much as possible but sometimes giving in and taking one or even two pills when the pressure got too much and I needed to deaden my senses for a while. It was such a dangerous coping strategy. I'd feel OK for a day or so and then suffer withdrawal symptoms the next, experiencing horrible headaches and bouts of bleak depression, or just feeling fidgety and fretful and not quite with it. I had a few panic attacks too. Not major ones where I thought I was going to die and needed an ambulance, but my breathing was out of control and I had to pace around outside and fight to regain my calm and breathe normally again.

Lucy and I had broken up many times, and one of our major problems was that I never thought I was good enough for her. She would always be super-devastated when we split up, and that was a huge pressure too. Now we started arguing every day. I obsessed constantly about my feelings, analysing the relationship, and I started to see that I loved Lucy as a person, but I wasn't in love with her any more. When I worked that out I knew I had to go it alone.

I broke up with Lucy about a week before boot camp, explaining to her that I needed time to focus on myself and my music. Even though it was painful for both of us I knew it was the right thing. I wasn't in love, and I didn't have the nervous capacity to deal with our relationship any longer.

*This is real. Get a grip. All you have to do is deliver your voice. Get it right. You can do this.*

This mantra was running constantly through my head and I knew what I had to do, but once I'd broken up with Lucy, my fear about the competition intensified. It meant that by the time I arrived at boot camp I was slipping so far into my anxiety I felt in danger of losing my grip on reality.

Boot camp was being held at the Liverpool Echo Arena that year and I got the train there on my own. When I arrived, there were about two hundred contestants milling around and the atmosphere was incredibly intense, right from the start. You couldn't move for bodies, the noise was insane and there were people randomly singing, everywhere. Lots of the contestants were 'on' the whole time, trying extremely hard to look good, sound good, stand out with their fashion sense, their voice – everything.

I was seriously worried about how I'd get through this. It was a three-day event and a part of me felt so stressed I wanted to turn and run. There were contracts to sign, producers to talk to, music choices to be discussed, conversations to be had about timings and stages and . . .

At one point my anxiety was raging so wildly I slipped out of the arena and hit myself in the face, really hard. I had to pull myself back from being lost to my nerves and this was how I tried to do it.

*This is real. SMACK! Get a grip. SMACK! All you have to do is deliver your voice. SMACK! Get it right. SMACK! You can do this, James.*

I had to sing as part of a group and on my own, and out of all the guys only six of us were going to make it through to judges' houses as solo performers. I was lucky to be put in a group with two really nice young lads, Curtis Golden and James Vickery, and we shared a hotel room too. There was a lot of partying going on around the place but the three of us knuckled down and worked hard on our performance all evening.

The next day we did The Fray's 'How to Save a Life' and it worked well. Tulisa was nodding and smiling right from the start and all the other judges looked impressed. Nevertheless, the tension was incredible. When I heard that we'd all survived to perform our solo songs I could feel the relief coursing through me.

I was singing Gary Barlow's 'A Million Love Songs' the next day. I figured it had worked well to do a Tulisa song last time, so hopefully now I could impress Gary with one of his songs. My version was a bit of a mad arrangement and it was quite long but I believed in it.

*I've got my act. I've got it down. I just need to be calm.*

That's what I told myself, non-stop. Looking around, a few singers stood out for me: Jahméne Douglas, Adam Burridge and Ella Henderson. This was a tough competition and I had a long way to go. Rylan Clark made an impression on me too – how could he not? He boosted the energy and turned heads every time he walked in a room.

*I've got my act. I've got it down. I just need to be calm.*

I was anticipating my performance every minute as I watched the mayhem around me. When it was finally my turn in front of the judges I was dripping with anxiety and emotion. It didn't help that I'd run out of contact lenses and had to wear my big NHS jam-jar glasses. People had been jokily teasing me, calling me Deirdre from *Coronation Street*. I knew I was not like any of the pretty boys in the bands and I wasn't a character like Rylan. My image and personality were not going to help me one bit; I had to put my heart and soul into my performance, because that's all I had.

'You know what, James, you made an amazing job of Tulisa's "Young" in your audition and you've done an incredible job of "A Million Love Songs". I think people are going to be writing to you requesting to be "James Arthured" because that was brilliant, well done.'

*Wild. Thank you again, Gary Barlow.*

I got another standing ovation. Tulisa said I had a 'Plan B vibe' about me, and as I left the room Nicole said, 'I love him.'

I was one of just twenty-four acts on my way to judges' houses. I felt pleased and proud of myself for about two minutes before my nerves re-plugged themselves in their usual super-sensitive, electrocuting way. Now I had another month to wait before judges' houses, and my immediate thought was that I didn't know how the hell I was going to cope.

*Avoid the spaces in between.*

I was facing another gap I couldn't avoid. I had to get through the next four weeks with my sanity intact and without falling through the cracks, but how?

It certainly wasn't easy. For one thing, I was homeless by this point. I hadn't done any gigs for a while because I was concentrating on *The X Factor* and I'd lost my bedsit because I couldn't pay the rent. I ended up staying on the sofa at Dawson's house. It wasn't ideal but I had nowhere else to go. His girlfriend was really fed up because we played *FIFA* on the PlayStation for hours on end, but I needed to keep myself busy, to stop the demons creeping into my head. I tried to occupy myself by rehearsing too, but the voices in my head chattered non-stop.

*Something's gonna go wrong. You're gonna get a call and they'll say they've made a mistake.*

When negative thoughts took hold I really struggled to stay calm and breathe normally. I felt super-messed up and thought I was losing my mind. I had a few panic attacks too, and so the week before judges' houses I went to the doctor and explained that my anxiety was through the roof and I needed help.

I was given Prozac. It was the first time I'd ever taken this brand of antidepressant and straight away it made me feel so wired and brought on all kinds of side effects. There was so much noise going on in my head that I felt even more crazy and anxious than before, and my jaw felt tight all the time. Then my heart started to race so much I felt like I was going to have a heart attack. At that point, I asked the doctor if I should stop taking the pills, but she said no, because they took a week to work and then I'd feel a lot better.

Thankfully she was right, because on the day I turned a corner and finally started to feel a bit calmer I was at Heathrow with all the other contestants, and we'd just been handed envelopes revealing our destination for judges' houses.

'We're going to Dubai!' Rylan shrieked. 'Actual Dubai!'

Rylan was so excited. He'd made the boys' category too, along with Adam, Jahméne, plus Jake Quickenden and Starboy Nathan. Other contestants were jumping up and down and screaming and laughing all around me. Everyone was buzzing and speculating about which judge would be their mentor but I couldn't speak. I felt paralysed and stayed rooted to the spot, silently running an old memory through my head.

*We're moving to Bahrain, son.*

I could hear Mam's words like I was back in the living room in Winchester Road, and I shrank straight back to the frightened nine-year-old boy I was then. Once again, I was leaving my old life behind and flying to the Middle East, and I was filled with terror and anxiety.

I had no idea how I was going to survive the journey.

# CHAPTER SEVEN

*I'm not worthless. I'm not just a scallywag.*
*I've got something to offer after all*

I was stunned when I saw the buildings and cars turn Lego-sized before disappearing magically beneath the clouds. I could hear the noise of the plane through my whistling ears and feel the unfamiliar bumps of turbulence under my seat. Flying was unbelievable. It was wild! I couldn't get over the fact I was actually in the sky, cruising above the earth.

When the seat-belt signs were switched off and I saw other passengers walking around it totally freaked me out. I didn't think you'd be allowed to get up and it looked so strange to see the sky moving behind people as they passed down the aisle. Me and Sian were wide-eyed and thinking this was so amazing. This was our first ever flight. We were actually on the way to the Middle East. This was a really big adventure, and even though I was still very wary about what life would be like from now on, this was undeniably exciting.

We were staying in Dubai for a couple of months before settling in Bahrain, because of Ronnie's job.

'I'll set up a tab for you,' he told Sian and me as we stood squinting in the baking heat. 'Get whatever you want.'

We looked at each other in astonishment. We'd landed in paradise, and now we were standing by the swimming pool of our hotel at the Dubai World Trade Centre. We'd gone from Redcar to Dubai overnight and it was totally mind-blowing. Instead of playing football in the street by the 'no ball games' sign, suddenly I was in my swimming trunks, ready to dive into the turquoise-blue pool and surrounded by palm trees and skyscrapers.

'Let's get some crisps,' Sian giggled.

'Come on! Let's get Fanta too.'

We went to the bar feeling like mini millionaires, and over the next few hours we ended up getting about ten packets of crisps and downing a dozen fizzy-orange Miranda drinks each, which we were fascinated by because they were luminous orange compared to the Fanta we had at home.

'Do you think the other kids will be nice when we get to Bahrain?' Sian said.

I'd been fretting about this a lot. Some of the boys at school had been really nasty, saying nobody would speak English and sneering that I'd be mixing with 'Pakis' and 'dirty Arabs'. I hated it when they said stuff like that, and I went absolutely mental one time when a boy used the 'n' word. I don't think racism was a word in my vocabulary when I was nine, but I was old enough to recognise prejudice and have a negative reaction to it. Every time a racist comment was made I'd experience a flush of hot anger rising up in my chest. I'd also feel confused, because I couldn't for the life of me see why the colour of a person's skin, or their religion, made them targets of hate like this. Where did these kids get it from? I couldn't understand it. Nothing like that was ever said in my house, by my family.

'Maybe we really will only have a camel for a friend,' I said.

Sian giggled. We'd had a running joke that we'd only have one friend in Bahrain, and he would be a camel called Humphrey.

'Me, you and Humphrey,' Sian said. 'We'll get along fine!'

It was my turn to laugh, albeit a bit nervously.

*What if it's true? Sian will be fine. Everybody likes Sian. She's normal, but what about me? I'm not like other kids. What if nobody likes me?*

I knew my little sister Jasmin would be fine too. She was still just a toddler and Mam and Ronnie doted on her. Ronnie called her 'bumblebee' and it was obvious Jazz was the apple of his eye. Sian and I were envious of her, to be honest, because she was Ronnie's clear favourite – understandably I guess, as he was her natural father – and he spoilt her rotten. I can't describe how many tantrums Jazz had, at every turn, but she always got her own way.

'Me first!' she'd say, wanting to get in the lift or the hotel room before anyone else.

If she didn't get her way she kicked off and created so much fuss it was unreal, so she always won, or at least that's how it appeared to me.

When we left Dubai and finally settled in Bahrain we lived in a gated compound called Miami Park that had a communal pool, a bowling alley and even a zoo. Our villa was huge compared to our house back home. We all had our own bedroom and private bathroom and there were glass chandeliers and marble floors. As Ronnie had promised, we had a housemaid too, who had her own quarters in the villa and did all the cleaning, so Mam didn't have to.

It was a very strange new world, but even though I was still a hyperactive and hyper-aware kid I settled into my new life much better than I ever expected to. It wasn't because of the pool, the wall-to-wall sunshine or our fancy new home. All that stuff is out of focus in my mind when I think back to Bahrain; it's the feelings I can remember most of all. I felt protected and happy most of the time, because Mam was happier than I'd ever seen her. I think she was gaining a lot of love and energy from seeing me and my sisters benefiting from the life out there, and she and Ronnie were still very loved up. I had a strong sense that we were all in this together. This was our family unit now: me, Sian, Jazz, Mam and Ronnie. We were tight-knit. Mam still shouted from time to time but she wasn't having a go at me nearly as much as she used to. Life was as good as I'd ever known it to be.

I went to the British School of Bahrain and I loved it, right from the start. I couldn't believe there was a kid from Marske in my class of twelve, as well as a lad from Leeds, and I was really interested to meet kids from all over the world. It was truly international, yet everybody had one thing in common: they respected one another. You didn't hear kids swearing and acting tough or bullying anyone. There were no 'chavs', as we said in Redcar, and on the way to school there were no streets you didn't want to walk down because you knew a kid wearing trackie bottoms and a scowl might have a go at you. The atmosphere was always pleasant and welcoming and inclusive, and I began to relax in my skin more than I ever had.

I loved drama classes, and when I was asked to play the part of the undertaker in the school production of *Oliver Twist* I jumped at the chance. I sang on stage in front of a proper audience for the first time ever, and I absolutely loved it. I'd never have had the bottle to do that back home, where singing and acting was considered 'poofy'. I'd have been too worried about being bullied to get on any stage in Redcar, but in Bahrain the drama department was well respected and I felt encouraged and empowered to follow my heart and have a go.

'I'm so proud of you,' Mam said after that show. She had been clapping and smiling in the audience, and it gave me a real buzz to see how genuinely thrilled she was to see me perform.

'I loved it,' I said. 'I want to do it again!'

'I'm not surprised, James, and you will. You're a natural. You're amazing.'

She talked about it for weeks, and I couldn't get enough of her praise.

The strange thing was that when I was performing I felt super-confident. It was like the fears and worries I carried with me all the time were temporarily disabled the moment I took a step on the stage. I did feel a few nerves in the moments before the curtain went up, but they were not debilitating or too intense. They gave me a healthy shot of adrenaline, and I felt on top of the world when I faced the audience.

It's a pattern that repeats even now, whenever I perform. I'm sure it's because I am in control of myself when I'm on stage. I know exactly what to do, and I know I have the ability, but most importantly I know I'll be heard, without anybody butting in and talking over me. Even if I'm in front of thousands of people I don't feel scared or exposed or self-conscious, because I am in charge. Not being able to control my situation is what always bothers me the most. Losing control is the scariest thing of all; that is something that has always knocked me off balance.

I was eventually asked to play the part of the Major-General in a production of *The Pirates of Penzance*. This was a big challenge because I had to sing that tongue-twister patter song, 'I am the very model of a modern Major-General'. I wasn't fazed at all; it was the opposite. I was buzzing and couldn't wait for the opening night, because I knew how good I would feel when I was on the stage singing.

Mam was absolutely bursting with pride again and she told everyone who would listen, 'That's my son! He's got a brilliant voice. He's a natural talent! He'll go far, you'll see!'

People came from all over the island to see the show. I got massive applause and I felt supercharged with energy and excitement. I stood on the stage in awe, looking at the audience, smiling for their cameras, soaking up the vibe and the energy and feeling so appreciated and happy and proud of myself. It was incredible. I'd never felt that good in my life before. I loved being backstage afterwards too, hanging out with my friends and feeling part of something special.

That night I had to stay in my mum's room because I was on such a high I couldn't settle and didn't want to go to bed.

'I can't sleep, Mam, I just want to keep talking about it! What the hell *was* that? That buzz is like nothing else. How can we get some more of it, Mam?'

She couldn't stop grinning either, and Ronnie was full of praise for me too. I was later named 'outstanding performer' and presented with the Island Weekly Award, which was a coveted talent award for kids that covered the whole of Bahrain. Now loads of people were saying I had a special talent, and I was starting to actually believe Mam when she told me I could really make something of this, and go on to be a singer or a Hollywood star. The praise and adulation went on for months.

*I'm not worthless. I'm not just a scallywag. I've got something to offer after all.*

That was how my brain processed and summed up my success: I wasn't worthless. I wasn't the little shit I'd been made to feel I was in the past. I guess a kid with greater self-esteem might have felt like a mini superstar, but that's not how it was. I was pleased I wasn't a loser after all, and I was relieved I had a place I could go to where I felt so good about myself, even just for a short time.

# CHAPTER EIGHT

*You look like an idiot. Everyone can see how much you're struggling. This is the end of the road*

'He sings like he doesn't have a choice. There's a pain there, a real pain.'

That's what Ne-Yo said to Nicole after I sang Bonnie Raitt's 'I Can't Make You Love Me' for them at judges' houses.

He was right. I had to sing because it was the only thing I had in my life, and I was in so much pain – emotional pain – it was untrue. I was the first boy up and I could feel the blood rushing all around my head; this was mind-bending.

From the minute I'd arrived in Dubai memories of my childhood had started coming through. The smell and intensity of the heat and humidity hit me straight away; it's an unmistakable vibe. I was back in the Middle East after more than a decade away, and that was as mind-bending as what I was doing there. I'd been plucked from obscurity and dropped into a shiny new world once again. Rags to riches, that was my story, back then and right now. But I knew the story didn't always end there; it hadn't last time.

*This is all going to go to shit. Why are you even bothering?*

I couldn't control the doom-mongering voices in my head. I was living on my nerves and on my Prozac tablets, and all the time I was trying to stay upright, look normal, appear sane.

Thank God for Rylan. He was so super-flamboyant he always managed to break the ice and make me smile and feel at ease. We were all staying in an incredibly luxurious hotel on the Palm Jumeirah. When we were first shown our private pool and beach and told we had personal butlers, Rylan had shrieked so much I thought he was going to pass out, and he was deliriously excited when Nicole sailed into the marina on a yacht, waving at us and looking absolutely stunning. I felt like a scruffy, introverted northern ape next to Rylan, but he never failed to make me laugh.

I liked all the boys who'd made it to judges' houses, in fact, and because there were a few eccentric characters in the group I felt OK around them. Jake was a cool guy, Adam and Nathan were both good lads and I really hit it off with Jahméne. I could see he suffered from nerves and didn't feel too comfortable in his skin either, so we had a connection there. Best of all, it felt like all the lads had each other's back, despite the fact only three of us would go through to the live shows.

The producers and crew were also a tonic. They were all super-kind and supportive and treated us all really well, praising us and helping us out as much as they could. One producer, Diccon, looked at me with genuine excitement when he heard me rehearsing, which gave me confidence. Caroline Flack was out there with us, and once I found my feet I started being flirty with her. I guess it was the old story with me; I've always loved women and been fascinated by them, and when I turn on the charm I somehow feel like a different person and discover a cockiness and confidence that isn't normally there. I thought Caroline was gorgeous and vivacious and I decided I had nothing to lose by trying to chat her up.

'You're beautiful,' I told her boldly, in front of the other boys when we were all around the pool one night, hanging out after we'd finished filming.

Caroline was giggling and I could see she'd taken a bit of a liking to me. After that there were genuinely a couple of moments between us when it felt like something might happen, if other people weren't there. It was fun and good for my self-esteem, even though afterwards, when I was alone in my hotel room, I sank straight back into a well of self-doubt.

I couldn't hide my unease when I finally went out to sing to Nicole and Ne-Yo. I felt like I had the most soulful song option of everyone and I'd practised hard, but I was struggling before I even opened my mouth. I'd just taken a dose of Prozac and it made me feel edgy and completely out of it. My nerves were knotting up all over my body and fear was grabbing at my throat. The Deirdre glasses were back as well, because I couldn't afford to buy any contact lenses, and they added to my paranoia.

*You look like an idiot. Everyone can see how much you're struggling. This is the end of the road.*

I held it together, just, though at the end of the song I felt so spent I thought I might die. Later, when I finally sat down on the sofa next to Nicole to hear whether I'd made it through to the live shows, I thought I was going to completely lose it. I was trying to look cool but my heart was pumping my blood so fast my face was hot and red, and my lungs were so tight and dry I couldn't get my breath in and out the way I wanted to.

'James, it's not good news.'

*Shit. No way. Don't cry.*

There was a long dramatic pause before a huge smile spread across Nicole's face and she started jumping up and down.

'It's freakin' amazing news!'

Suddenly I was hugging Nicole and telling her I couldn't believe she'd done this for me. I couldn't believe any of this was happening. I was through to the live shows. It *was* freakin' amazing news, but straight away I started to panic about the next step. I also had to navigate another gap in the process, because the lives didn't start for more than a month. I honestly didn't know if my nerves could take it.

*The cracks in between. You can't do it, James. This is going to end in tears.*

A day or two later I was back on the familiar pavements of home, with nothing to do all day but think about my next performance – live on TV. I had an added worry in my life now too. My Newcastle audition had been broadcast and it had blown up in a big way, which meant I was already a minor celebrity in my home town. Strangers were starting to talk to me in the corner shop and I was featured in the local paper. It was just so weird, and I could feel my fear mounting.

I was still homeless, and I went back to sleeping on Dawson's sofa. At night, I'd lie there alone and dwell on all the pressure I was under, worrying incessantly about how I was going to deal with it. I was the matchstick snapping under the slabs of meat, the toothpick being crushed under the piles of papers. I had to up my game. I had to give myself the best possible chance or I was going to bend and break.

I came off the Prozac and went back to taking Sertraline. As it was the antidepressant I'd taken for years, it worked better for me and I knew more about it. I'd learned that Sertraline is what's known as an SSRI – a selective serotonin reuptake inhibitor – and it works by boosting levels of the neurotransmitter serotonin in the brain. A rise in serotonin levels is thought to have a positive influence on your mood, emotion and sleep, although there is a lot of research still to be done into precisely why.

There are loads of possible side effects of the drug, including feeling agitated, shaky or anxious and having problems sleeping. My usual habit was to self-medicate those negative symptoms by smoking weed, but I knew I couldn't do *The X Factor* on marijuana and I didn't want to: the fear of being caught and thrown off the show, or appearing stoned on television, was unthinkable. It meant I was stuck with just the Sertraline, and as soon as I took it again it lifted me the right side of depression but also did what it had done before when I took it in isolation: it made me feel a bit numb and disconnected from the world. I was glad to be released from my wild nerves and severe anxiety, but there were no highs or lows at all. It was obvious that Sertraline was suspending me in a state of deadened emotions, and I began a new wave of worry.

*This drug is suppressing my creativity. I can't do* The X Factor *feeling numb. What if the producers find out I'm on antidepressants? They might kick me off the show. All this work will be for nothing. Everybody will know the truth. I'm not normal. What happens in my head isn't right.*

Just before the live shows I got myself into such a state of paranoia about the stigma and the side effects that I decided the Sertraline had to go, once and for all. I had to get rid of the secret and I had to give myself the best possible chance of success. The trouble was, once again I didn't come off the drug as you are meant to. I'd left it too late to wean myself off by gradually reducing the dose and carefully monitoring my progress. Instead I messed around with the dose for a week or so and then, on the eve of the live shows, I threw all the pills in the bin and decided to go it alone.

'Oooh, James! There's a phone in the bathroom, babe!'

I was sharing a room with Rylan at the *X Factor* hotel in London. We'd just arrived and were having a look around, with a camera following us.

'Sick, man,' I replied.

I think we'd been put together as roommates for the comedy element because we were like chalk and cheese, and the producers could probably see the potential for some fun. I was pleased they had because Rylan was a great antidote to my nerves.

'Can you put some clothes on?' I'd say daily. 'I'm seeing more of your penis than my own!'

We laughed a lot, and right from the start Rylan was very kind and warm and supportive, especially when he could see

I was anxious or a bit down. Our hotel room became a refuge from the *X Factor* studios, where the atmosphere was completely wild and super-intense all the time.

When we went to start rehearsals for our first performance it was like stepping into another universe and I was surrounded by so much chatter, inside and outside my head, it was insane.

'James, Nicole wants to see you in her dressing room. James, can you have a chat with Dermot for a second? James, you need to go to a debrief with Rylan and Jahméne. James, you need to go to the choreography room. James, James, James . . .'

*Yep, yep, yep. I'll do it. I feel like my head's gonna explode but I'll do it.*

I was trying to give everyone what they wanted and it was exhausting. I should have been more sparing with my energy, but I didn't know the game. I was in full-on fight mode, on high alert, trying to be super-switched on but struggling like mad. I didn't ever feel normal, but I don't think anyone could in such a fraught situation.

Every day was like a series of mind-blowing events. We went on breakfast TV, we gave press interviews and did photo shoots and I was bumping into people like Gary and Tulisa in the corridor. Nicole and I hit it off really well and she was becoming my best friend, which was just bizarre. I couldn't get over her. She gave so much of herself, and I identified with her in a way I didn't expect. I think she saw something of herself in me too, because she has issues and is really tortured as well – much more than she ever lets on. I was fascinated by how beautiful she is, and the boy inside me was always subtly flirting with her, imagining we might have a romance.

The minute-by-minute pressure was so immense that fear always trumped any feeling of excitement I experienced. I also had the added stress of coping without my antidepressants. I had no pills in my pocket, just at the time when I most needed to reach for one, and that was freaking me out and making me feel super-vulnerable.

I was shitting it when I went out on stage for my first live performance, singing Kelly Clarkson's 'Stronger'. It was such an ironic song choice because I didn't feel strong in any way. I felt incredibly uncomfortable in my own skin, and all of this at a time when every flaw was being picked over. Not only was I being scrutinised by the judges, everything about me was suddenly in the spotlight and open to public criticism: my eyes, my teeth, my tattoos, my clothes, my voice, my song choices, my attitude, the way I talked, the way I moved, the way I blinked.

I'd already been trolled online and I'd made the mistake of searching through Twitter and reading some of the nasty things people said about my appearance. I was convinced you could see my bong-eye when I stepped on stage, and I was so worried about people seeing my teeth that I held back vocally, trying to keep my mouth closed as much as possible, to limit the negative comments I'd inevitably get afterwards.

I didn't do myself justice vocally in my first performance and I looked like an idiot with my hair in a big quiff. Gary gave me the only negative comment I got in the whole competition, saying I needed to retain my integrity. He was right. I thought I was absolutely terrible. I wished I could sing my song all over again, giving one hundred per cent to show what I really could do, but a massive amount of my energy was going into trying to hide my terror. When I survived to week two I felt like I'd robbed the bank.

I wasn't the only one buckling under the pressure. Rylan was devastated because he was being viewed as the novelty act, even though he can sing. He divided the nation and Gary was giving him stick, which really upset him. Jahméne was also struggling with nerves and anxiety like me, but the three of us pulled together, supporting each other and bigging each other up like a band of brothers.

In the hotel, I often composed little songs on the acoustic guitar, and one night I wrote one called 'Rylander, the saviour of the universe', just for a laugh. Rylan wanted to collaborate so we popped in a little verse for him to sing, and I'd go, 'One, two, three, Rylan's verse' to cue him to do his bit. He loved it so much and was forever saying, 'Play that song for me again, babe!' Funny moments like that, and the support I got from the boys, Nicole and so many other people backstage, rescued me a lot. The other positive was that I never, ever stopped believing in my voice, even though I was completely paranoid about everything else.

*You're an oddball. You're a weirdo. You're gonna be terrible when you get on stage. The song isn't right. You're gonna collapse. You're gonna lose it, in front of the whole nation.*

The demons were screaming at me when I stepped out to perform 'No More Drama' in week two. Nicole had fixed it for me to talk to Mary J. Blige on the phone and she'd wished me luck. It was incredible to speak to her, but it piled on the pressure too. I went white when I started singing, and I was feeling the song so much it was exhausting.

*You're gonna collapse. You're gonna lose it, in front of the whole nation.*

The audience was screaming at me now too, and suddenly the judges were giving me great comments, drowning out the negative chatter in my head at long last. I didn't know what to say. I had to get off the stage and I had to breathe. The whole experience was too much for me, and no matter how hard I tried to catch my breath and get my heart to beat at a normal pace, I couldn't compose myself.

*Someone please call me an ambulance. I need an ambulance, right now. I'm having a heart attack. I'm going to die.*

This was the night I had the panic attack backstage, and I truly believed I was going to die. That's the awful thing about panic attacks. No matter how many times you have one, and how many times you come out the other end, you always think that this is the one that's going to kill you.

When the attack eventually subsided, I felt relieved but also very embarrassed, and I wanted to do what I always did in the past when anxiety got too much for me. I wanted to be on my own, to disappear, to lock myself away from the world. I wanted to self-medicate with weed or antidepressant pills or alcohol, or some mixture of them all. I wanted to numb my brain and fall into oblivion, because that's all I could cope with until I got my breath back – properly back – and until I felt strong enough to face some kind of reality again.

But I couldn't take flight this time, and that reality was terrifying. I'd beaten tens of thousands of other hopefuls to claim a place in these live shows. I was one of just thirteen acts who'd got this far and had the chance to showcase their talent in front of the nation and win a record deal with Syco. I couldn't throw it all away now. However impossible it seemed in that moment, I knew I had to dig deep and keep going. My mum and dad and sisters were all rooting for me. I had to prove to myself and to all the family and friends who'd supported me that I could actually do what I'd said I could do for as long as I could remember. If I ran away, then what?

What the hell would happen to me? I knew I had to try to stay in control, but I didn't know if I could.

The day after my panic attack I put out a short statement to the media, as it had not gone unnoticed that an ambulance had been called to the *X Factor* studios after I went off stage. The press had speculated that I'd had a 'collapse' and there were photographs of Nicole and Rylan standing beside me and the paramedics, looking anxious.

'I feel loads better this morning after a good night's sleep,' I said, confirming that I'd suffered an anxiety attack and adding I would still be appearing on the results show. 'I'm looking forward to tonight's show – there's no way I'm missing it.'

That was it; the die was cast. I'd declared to myself and the public I was not going to be beaten by anxiety, and I was not going to run away and hide.

I tried to be brave and positive about this decision, telling myself that this was meant to be my fairy tale, my rags-to-riches success story. I desperately wanted to believe in my own story and finally get my reward for all the pain I'd gone through in the past, but the truth was I had no idea if my nerves were strong enough.

As I prepared for the results show the next day I kept thinking about what I'd said: *I'm looking forward to tonight's show*. I wasn't looking forward to it at all. This was a necessary lie I told to the people who watched the show, and to myself, to a certain extent. It's what I wanted to believe, what I had to try to believe, because wasn't that a normal way to think and feel about appearing on one of the biggest talent shows in the world? Wouldn't a normal person feel more excited than daunted about the show, and be filled with anticipation rather than abject dread and fear? I wished I was normal like everybody else, but this was something that had evaded me my whole life.

At best I was weird, at worst I was on the edge of going completely crazy.

# CHAPTER NINE

## *I'm not going crazy. I'm not losing my mind*

'I'm too homesick,' Mam cried. 'I want to go back to Redcar.'

It was 2000 and we'd been living in Bahrain for three years. My little sister Neve had been born out there that summer when Sian was thirteen, I was twelve and Jasmin was five.

I'd built a very good life for myself and was happy, or at least as happy as I'd ever been, because I have never been what I would describe as 'blissfully' happy. Anyhow, I had plenty of friends, I was popular with the girls, I was in a football team and most of all I felt I belonged and wasn't such an oddball as I'd been in Redcar.

I was still the class clown because I knew he was a character who was accepted by the other kids at school, but even so I was doing much better academically than I did back home. The drama classes really engaged me, I loved English and creative writing and I generally felt more worldly-wise. I had friends from Saudi Arabia, Pakistan and from all around Europe and America. They were cultured and kind and pleasant to be around. I always wanted to fit in rather than stand out, and as a result I'd become less rough around the edges. Even my strong Middlesbrough accent softened, so much so that I won the 'Best Speaker' award in the school's 'Eloquent English' competition.

'Why are you homesick, Mam?'

I was genuinely confused. We were living in paradise, and everything we had here was way better than back home.

'It's the lifestyle. I miss having friends pop in for a cup of tea. If I want to see anyone I have to arrange to go out for a dinner or something. It's not the same.'

When I stopped and thought about it I realised Mam must have been lonely. Me and Sian were out at school all day and Mam spent a lot of time on her own with my two little sisters. It must have been hard, having a new baby and coping with Jasmin, who was always such a handful. Jazz was not only hyperactive but super-intelligent too, and the combination meant she was one of those kids you could never take your eye off for a second. Even though I was still very hyper myself, Jazz's energy, willpower and sheer force of personality made me catch my breath. She was crazy and awesome and I admired her and loved her to bits, but she was always totally exhausting and nerve-racking to be around too.

I was really into watching WWE wrestling on the TV and I'd come home from school and be glued to it. I'd jump on the bed doing body slams, pretending I was The Rock, Stone Cold Steve Austin or Triple H. If Jasmin came in my room I'd slam her on the bed doing 'rock bottoms'.

'Stop it, Jamie,' she'd squeal, but she loved it really. We were as bad as each other.

Mam would shout at us to calm down and tell us we were an accident waiting to happen but the truth is, I was an accident waiting to happen when I *wasn't* distracted or immersed in something or other, because then I over-thought my life and allowed worries to flood in. That's why the life I had in Bahrain worked so well for me, because there was so much to occupy me.

Ronnie was out at work all the time, although he did make a big effort with all the family whenever he was around. As far as I could see, he doted on Mam and did his very best to make her happy.

There was a sports club on our compound and Ronnie would take me there to watch the Middlesbrough games on Sky. I thought it was incredible we could watch the match from halfway around the world, and it would be the highlight of my week whenever I went to the club with Ronnie. We'd watch the afternoon matches live in the evening, and I absolutely loved it.

I started calling Ronnie 'Dad' in Bahrain. It was what Mam wanted, and from the moment we moved there she drilled it into Sian and me that Ronnie was our dad now. We even took his surname, tagging it on to the end of our names, so I was known as James Arthur-Rafferty. Mam said we had to do that because of the rules in Bahrain, and I accepted it and even took on the nickname 'Raff' with my mates.

'How are things with your mam?' Ronnie would ask in between chats about the football.

He was genuinely interested in my well-being and sensitive to the fact I was away from my dad, and I appreciated him asking.

'OK,' I'd shrug, 'but I do feel she has it in for me sometimes . . .'

I think Ronnie could see that my mum could treat me unfairly. We still bickered a lot and, whatever mood she was in, I was permanently on my guard around Mam because if anything annoyed her she would snap real quick. She was super-sensitive and so was I, which was a lethal combination. If the tiniest thing wasn't right, Mam would go off on one in a really over-the-top way, and I would take everything she said to heart, which was devastating.

'Don't get on your mum's bad side, James,' Ronnie would say. 'It's just not worth it, do you understand?'

I understood this all too well. I felt Mam didn't listen. I felt I wasn't being heard. Mam was way too quick to snap before hearing me out, and I was scared of her moods.

'But why is she being like that?' I asked one time, after Mam flew off the handle about something really trivial, like how I ignored her when I just hadn't heard her, or why she hadn't been the first to hear about such-and-such.

'The problem is she's wrapped up in herself, in a world of self-image,' Ronnie replied, adding that she was never going to change. I remember feeling so relieved to have a smart man like Ronnie acknowledge that things weren't right with Mam.

*I'm not going crazy. I'm not losing my mind. It's not fair, the way Mam treats me.*

I knew Ronnie had my back and I was very grateful for the way he looked out for me, but because he wasn't my real dad I always felt a bit unsure about how much stuff I could talk to him about. I was becoming a teenager and having major crushes on girls, but I didn't feel I could discuss that kind of thing with Ronnie. My body was changing and I put on a bit of weight and became chubby. It was odd to me to experience this as I'd always been a skinny kid. It would have been good to talk about this stuff, but I never did.

I never talked to Mam about puberty or personal issues either. She's such an open person and I'd hear her telling all kinds of tales to her friends, usually in a dramatic way. I didn't want her to discuss any of my private life with other people or with Sian, so I kept quiet.

My dad did his best to call us from England but Mam would always kick off when he tried to get through. I think I only ever managed to speak to him about once a year, always with Mam going mad in the background. Even so it was good to hear Dad's familiar, gentle Scottish accent. I missed him and wanted to keep in touch, but I always ended up feeling super-anxious. Hearing Mam shouting about him like a wild woman made me feel like I'd slipped through a time tunnel and been spat out in Redcar in the mid-nineties, with Mam doing all she could to derail our visits to Dad.

Apparently, the whole family went back to the UK once a year, but strangely I have no recollection of the three or four trips we made. Seeing my dad and my sister Charlotte after being away for so long must have been big events in my life, but I can only assume the visits created so much drama and bitterness between my parents that I've blocked them out, to push the trauma away.

Other memories from that time are incredibly vivid.

'Come quick!' I called to Ronnie. 'I can see those faces again!'

My bedroom in Bahrain was really cool. I had a big double bed, my own TV and a view of palm trees, but I had the same problem with the walls I'd had in my little bedroom in Redcar. Faces appeared at night. They morphed out of my bedroom walls like pictures coming to life in a horror film, or sometimes they burst into my eyes with flashes of white light.

Every night I insisted on having the air conditioning in my room set on maximum so it was absolutely freezing, like in England. I always found the heat and humidity hard to handle and I couldn't sleep if my room wasn't ice-cold, although I still woke up a lot during the night and saw the faces. I was a sleepwalker too.

'It's OK, James. It's just a nightmare.'

This is what Ronnie always said when I told him I saw the faces in the walls or flashing in my eyes, but I knew it wasn't a nightmare. They were real, and I saw them when I was wide awake, not in the middle of a bad dream when I was asleep. I also heard voices sometimes, which totally freaked me out because I thought I was going mad, or that someone was coming to get me.

I eventually told this to Mam one day because I was so terrified. I remember it well, because she went very quiet and listened, like she was really concerned and interested in what I was saying.

'What sort of voices, James?'

'Just voices. People saying stuff. I don't know who they are. I don't want them to talk to me, but they do.'

'What are they saying?'

'I don't know. It sounds like they are shouting something. They are saying weird stuff. I can't remember.'

After that Mam took me to see a neurologist at the Bahrain International Hospital. She explained everything about me hearing voices, sleepwalking and insisting on sleeping in an ice-cold room, and she also told the doctor my birth had been traumatic. Mam had an epidural that went terribly wrong, I was in distress in the womb for three hours and we both nearly died before I was delivered by caesarean. I ended up in special care with doctors warning I might be left with problems with my breathing, hearing, sight and speech.

'For the first year of James' life he slept like an angel, all the time, and never cried,' Mam explained. 'It was like he needed to sleep to get over the trauma of his birth, and then after that he became incredibly hyperactive, from about the age of two.'

The neurologist asked me to write a letter, and he later told my mum there was a lot of dark stuff in it. I was referred to a child psychologist who queried whether I had childhood schizophrenia and recommended I had an MRI scan, but this didn't happen. Ronnie was adamant I was just a kid having night terrors and would grow out of them, and he was also worried about giving me a label that might stigmatise me.

Mam reluctantly listened to Ronnie, which she later regretted. She tried to reason that my problems could have been caused by a triple operation I'd had at the age of ten. After a very serious bout of tonsillitis I had my tonsils removed, and during the same operation I also had my adenoids taken out and grommets inserted. This was another major trauma for me, and Mam thought that having all three surgeries at once could have caused a build-up of pressure in my head. She also thought my insistence on sleeping in freezing temperatures might have been due to the fact my various ailments caused me to have a lot of fevers. Either way, I never had the scan and I kept hearing voices throughout my childhood.

When Mam got homesick I began to suffer from a lot of anxiety. She would still put on Stevie Wonder or Michael Jackson when she was cooking and I'd see glimpses of my positive, vivacious mum when she sang along, but something had shifted. Gloom had started to descend on her, in waves, and I became her scapegoat again.

'Look at me when I'm speaking to you!'

She was suddenly screeching at me like I'd committed murder.

'What? Calm down, I didn't even know you were talking to me, Mam . . .'

'Don't give me cheek! What do you ever do to help me? Nobody knows what my life is like! All I ever hear is the worst word from your mouth . . .'

It didn't matter what I did or said to try to appease her, Mam got louder and angrier, criticising me about anything that came into her head.

'You're just like your dad! I wish you'd never been born!'

That was her hand grenade. She threw it at me to make sure I exploded. Then she got the angry argument she wanted, the justification for her cruel words.

'You're bored and lonely, Mam, and you're taking it out on me! You've just got it in for me for no reason! I hate you!'

I'd kick a chair or slam a door, and Mam would jump on that. 'See! What did I tell you? Just like your father!'

I began to wonder if Mam was jealous of the life I had. I was so settled and always had something going on. I had a great circle of friends in and out of school, and I'd even got myself a beautiful girlfriend called Amira. I adored her, and the fact she was interested in me was amazing and gave my confidence a boost. I wanted to be happy, but the more Mam struggled with her loneliness and homesickness, the more I lived on my nerves. Every day I was hyper-alert about Mam's mood, because I knew that whatever she was feeling would be transmitted to me.

One day Mam played No Doubt's 'Don't Speak' in the house and started crying. Her mood enveloped mine. It was like we were threaded together by our emotions and I had no escape, because when Mam started to drop she pulled me down with her. The song title was so apt. Mam didn't have to speak to me to tell me what was going on in her head. This track reminded us both of home, of friends we had left behind, the life we'd let go. She must have played it a hundred times, and she did the same with a Shania Twain album, playing the same sentimental tracks over and over again when she took me out for a drive. Mam loved driving. She'd passed her test out there, and we spent hours together, driving and listening to music.

I empathised with Mam so much. I could see how much pain she was in, but I didn't want to leave the life I had in Bahrain. Waving goodbye to my amazing life and going back to Redcar was unthinkable. The thought of leaving Amira killed me. Being pulled back into the clouds with Mam terrified me.

# CHAPTER TEN

## Who even are you? You better find out quick, James, or you'll get lost

'I'm prescribing you the antidepressant Sertraline, the tranquilliser Diazepam to calm your anxiety, plus sleeping tablets so you can get some rest.'

'Thank you so, so much.'

Relief flooded me and I couldn't wait to swallow the pills. A doctor had examined me following my panic attack backstage and this combination of drugs was what she thought was best to help me cope. It seemed a lot to take but I didn't argue at all. I needed help, and I was desperate not to have a panic attack on stage, in front of millions of viewers. That was a real possibility without the drugs to knock the edges off my fears and worries, and it was something I obviously couldn't risk. Just the thought of it filled me with heart-racing terror, and so I took the drugs willingly, every single one of them.

I was very grateful I hadn't been thrown off the show or stigmatised as I thought I would be. There was a pastoral care lady behind the scenes, 'Welfare Clare' we called her. She was very understanding and kept an eye on me, and Nicole and the producers were all looking out for me, doing their very best to keep me on track. The pills were a lifeline – or at least a lifeline of sorts.

'Come on, big bro. Wake up! You're gonna go out there and blow everyone away again. Get up!'

It was minutes before I was due on stage and Ella Henderson was trying to wake me up.

'Ella, babe, I'll do my best but I'm not with it.'

Ella and I had hit it off from the start of the competition. She was only sixteen, her voice was amazing and I was so impressed by her. I thought she was the one who could win it, but even so she would often come to me for advice, which is how she started calling me 'big bro'. After my panic attack, the roles changed. All I wanted to do was sleep, and Ella would always be there, telling me how good I was and dragging me to my feet.

It was a real struggle. The drugs had done their job, in that my anxiety was under control, but there was a heavy price to pay. From week three of the live shows I was so out of it I felt zombified the whole time. If I wasn't sleeping, I was eating. I started smashing the canteen food and generally slobbing around. I was about twelve and a half stone when I started on *The X Factor*, which was a good weight for me, as I'm six foot three. Now my weight was shooting up, and in just a few weeks I hit sixteen stone. I looked like shit, and I'd roll up to rehearsals with a really bolshie attitude.

'I'm not doing that bullshit,' I'd say to the producers, or even to Nicole sometimes.

I'm naturally very competitive and I cared about my song choices even though I felt like a zombie. I didn't want to be in a position where Gary was saying I'd compromised my integrity ever again. I had to show everyone I was still in the game, fighting to win, but the truth was I felt so spaced out it was untrue, and I was working very hard at just trying to appear normal.

On stage I wasn't just performing below a hundred per cent, like in the first couple of weeks. Now I was scraping by at probably about thirty per cent, if that. My basic ability got me through every week, but it was such a painful experience because I knew I was significantly better than the version of myself I was displaying on the show.

All my memories of the competition are blurred from this point on. When I try to cast my mind back and piece it all together it's incredibly hard. It's not just that I was out of it on all the prescription drugs, but also because remembering the pressure I was under triggers major anxiety. Just imagining myself back in the *X Factor* studio makes my heart race and my breath catch in my throat.

Having said all that, there are some moments I won't ever forget.

Singing to Robbie Williams was one of them, when he was guest mentor. I was swallowed up by his aura when I walked in the room for a practice session with him. He was full of life and energy while I stood there awkwardly. It was just me, Robbie and a piano. It was such a privilege but at the same time it was my worst nightmare and I couldn't look him in the eye.

'What's up, man?' Robbie asked. 'Where's the confidence?' He was staring at me intensely.

'You're fucking Robbie Williams! You can't expect me to give you an honest performance. When I get on stage for a live show I come alive, but I can't perform in this scenario. I can't do it.'

Generously, Robbie changed the subject to talking about the fact we both had 'love' and 'life' tattooed across our knuckles, and we had a fist pump, which broke the ice a bit. When I left the room, I was so relieved. Robbie said good luck and I had no idea if he really liked me or hated me. Still, I'd met another legend – he's a god just like Gary in my eyes.

It was always a buzz seeing amazing singers on the show. I walked past Pink backstage one day and nearly lost my mind. Meeting Gwen Stefani was incredible too. It took me back to listening to 'Don't Speak' with my mum in Bahrain, and that's why I chose to perform the track in week five, because it meant such a lot to me. When Ed Sheeran came on the show I felt a connection to him and we hit it off straight away – we're still mates now. Ed said I was his favourite contestant, and all the guest artists were starting to say the same thing. I was always grateful, but at the same time I'd cringe because I felt so anxious already, and their praise piled more pressure on me.

The funny moments stand out for me too. The last six acts left in the competition were taken to Disneyland Paris, to celebrate the park's twentieth anniversary. I was never into publicity stunts and everyone on the show knew this and let me avoid a lot of that kind of stuff, but I couldn't get out of this.

'Come on babe, put these on,' Rylan said, thrusting a pair of fluffy Mickey Mouse ears at me.

'Are you kidding? Am I fuck wearing those!'

Rylan was always good at reminding me not to take myself too seriously, without actually saying anything. In the end, I not only put on the ears but I carried a balloon and let Rylan put his arm round me. Then we were photographed walking round holding hands like girlfriend and boyfriend, with me laughing and saying, 'Have you seen me? What did Gary say about keeping my integrity . . . ?'

I had a few funny moments with Tulisa too. Having spotted I was shitting it backstage one night she took me in her dressing room and said she had something that would help.

'Have this,' she said. 'It'll take the edge off.'

I swigged the shot of Jack Daniels and it worked at first, but then when I was on stage my heart started going absolutely crazy. I remember looking at Tulisa and thinking, 'I *really* wish I hadn't done that. I'm staying away from your dressing room from now on.'

Ella once asked Tulisa which of the boys on the show she would fancy, and Tulisa answered, 'I like chavvy guys, so I'd probably say James.' When Ella told me this I made a point of flirting with Tulisa every time I saw her. 'Alright Tulisa, you're looking good today,' I'd say when I saw her in the corridor. 'When are you gonna let me take you out on that date?' I think she liked it – there was a good vibe between us and it always gave us both a smile.

My flirting with Caroline Flack was on another level altogether. I chatted her up very openly when I went on *The Xtra Factor*, so much so that it almost became a segment of the show, and a compilation video called 'James Arthur and Caroline Flack – A Flirting Master-Class' ended up on YouTube. My campaign actually worked, because Caroline and I eventually met up a few times, after the show ended. We shared a few kisses but not a lot more than that, and in the end our little romance fizzled out. I think we were both so busy it was never going to work.

Crazy things were happening to me and the pressure was building every week as I progressed through the competition. In week seven I ended up in the bottom two with Ella. It's hard to get a handle on what the public is thinking when you are in the *X Factor* bubble, but it felt like Ella was the favourite to win, the clear front runner. I'd always secretly thought I was that guy who would probably go out in week six, so when we were in the bottom two together I was sure I was a goner. No way was I beating Ella.

As we waited to see who was being eliminated I stood there telling myself not to crack or pass out. I felt sick, not only about what would happen that night but how this might affect my whole future. I was dying inside, and all my confidence was shrinking away.

*Face it. This is it. You are not good enough. Nobody wants you here any more. You're getting thrown out. You'll be off the show. You'll lose your* X Factor *friends. You'll be homeless, out in the cold. That is your life.*

I was stunned when I was saved by the public vote, and this became a big turning point for me. I instantly got fire in my belly, like never before, and I told everyone who would listen that I absolutely needed to win the show now Ella was gone.

'You have to do everything you can to help me win,' I said to production. 'We need to work together.'

Even though I was still drugged up and didn't have much energy I tried to put much more effort into the routines and I was all over my song choices, looking for ways I could stand out musically. For Abba week I thought, 'How the hell am I going to do that?' and then I thought, 'Right, this is how. I'll do "SOS" with a Kurt Cobain verse and a Fat Boy Slim chorus.' It worked, even though by now I was flagging so much I reckon I was only operating at about twenty per cent. I kept up the same attitude and used the same tactics all the way through to the final, and every week I had the same thought: 'I've robbed the bank again.'

There was another event that made me come out fighting. Frankie Boyle made offensive remarks about me and Jahméne on Twitter, and when I snapped and tweeted he was 'about as funny as Aids' I got a lot of stick for it. I was furious, because I couldn't understand why anybody would support a man who was so offensive, and famous for making jokes about disabled kids.

In hindsight, I was easy prey and I should never have bitten when I was provoked, but where I come from you defend yourself when somebody attacks you. Thankfully, I think the Twitter spat ultimately made me more determined to come out on top and prove I was a winner, and the only way to do that was through my performances. I didn't want fame; nonsense like this proved how dangerous and unfulfilling it could be. But I desperately wanted my music to be recognised, and to be able to earn my living from being a credible artist. There was nothing else in the world I wanted more.

'Rita wants to meet you,' a cameraman said to me one night.

I'd just come off stage and was still coming down.

'Sorry, what? Rita Ora wants to meet *me*?'

Rita had been a guest on the show and I'd watched her in awe. I thought she was gorgeous. Only months earlier I was watching her music videos in my bedsit, getting hot under the collar. This was the stuff of fairy tales; my life was insane. I'd recently been reminded of just how dramatically my life had changed when I went back to my bedsit with a TV crew to film shots for my homecoming video, as all finalists do.

When the crew squeezed into the poky room they were shocked and visibly moved. They couldn't believe how small and sad the bedsit was, or that I shared a toilet down the hall with six other men. One of the crew told me afterwards he'd never seen anything like it in his life; he thought it looked like a prison cell. Nicole was with us, and she burst out crying.

'This is my life, don't worry about it,' I shrugged. Still, it was impossible not to view my situation in a different light now, having gone through this process and stepped into a totally different world.

I went to meet Rita backstage and I was blown away by her. She was like a throwback to an old film star and she was *so* flirtatious. I'd never experienced anything like that incredible confidence in a woman before. I thought to myself I had to match this and try to be cool, or I'd end up looking like some silly little boy. I think I must have held my own, because unbelievably we swapped numbers. It was wild. I was living a dream as well as a nightmare.

When I made it to the final with Jahméne it felt so surreal to be there. He did 'Angels' and 'Let It Be' and I did 'Let's Get It On' and Shontelle's 'Impossible'. I'd had a huge panic in rehearsals because I lost my voice when I did 'Impossible'. I always overdid it in the sound checks, wanting to impress everyone because I was so competitive. It nearly cost me dear, but I got away with it. My final performance was not my best, but I was just glad to get through it without any part of me collapsing.

Strangely, when me and Jahméne were standing on the stage, waiting for the final result, I looked around and had a very strong feeling that this wasn't it. Whatever happened, this was not my defining moment. I just knew it, and Jahméne has since told me he felt the same way. I was wired but weirdly disconnected at the same time. It was like anxiously awaiting an anticlimax.

*Even if you win this isn't it. It won't make up for all the years of feeling lonely and cast aside.*

'The winner of *The X Factor* 2012 is . . . James Arthur.'

I barely smiled. This was so unfulfilling, and I didn't have a clue what to say.

*This should be your crowning glory. You've finally arrived in the world, or have you? Who even are you? You better find out quick, James, or you'll get lost.*

I only just managed to sing my winner's single. 'Impossible' is an incredibly hard song to sing, especially the version we came up with, and on the last chorus I was practically scream-ing: 'Tell them I was happy, and my heart is broken, all my scars are open, tell them what I hoped would be impossible.'

It *was* impossible. I was surrounded by all the other contest-ants, there was glitter falling from the ceiling, lights strobing all around me and Nicole was out of her seat, running up to hug me on stage. I should have felt complete, but I didn't. My scars were open, in my head, but nobody could see them or the pain and damage they caused me.

I was spent, and the after-show party is a blur. There were loads of media people and it felt like everyone wanted a picture. The vibe was so crazy and I couldn't take it in at all. 'You're amazing,' Mam said, as she did after every performance. She was my biggest fan and was always bursting with pride, but there were lots of times when I looked at her, and my dad, and felt nothing towards them, or I felt resentment. I had no idea how to communicate with them on this kind of level. I'd never talked about pride and stuff like that with my parents, and they felt like strangers who had no idea who I was or what I was going through.

*Why didn't you support me when I needed you most? It's too late. I'm too damaged. Where were you when I was a kid?*

That voice wouldn't stop tormenting me, but ultimately, I was thankful Mam and Dad were there for me now, and I felt full of gratitude to them both for educating me about music over the years. I would not have been on that stage if it wasn't for them. I think my emotions were flattened by the cocktail of drugs I was on, and I felt so fraught that the negative voices were booming loud in my head, despite the celebrations all around me.

*You can't erase the past. You're still the same misfit you always were. You've won the show but who the hell are you?*

When I was finally alone at the hotel, trying to snatch some sleep before going on TV the next morning, I felt super-lonely. I had nobody to share this with and I felt as scared and anxious as I did as a little boy, crying into my pillow.

# CHAPTER ELEVEN

*What more can go wrong? Life is so confusing*

I blinked and my whole world changed, that's how it felt. I was in the clouds, but they weren't the metaphorical clouds that were Mam's black moods. I was actually strapped into an airline seat. Flying back to England. For good.

I sobbed my heart out. Amira had finally professed her love for me two days earlier. 'I love you, James,' she said, and those words filled me with so much joy. I loved Bahrain. I had a beautiful girlfriend, lots of friends and I fitted in. I didn't want this feeling to end, but I knew that when I got back to

Middlesbrough it would. I'd be plunged back into my old life, where I was already a misfit before I became 'desert boy'. What the hell was it going to be like now? Who even was I? And how could I live without Amira?

My girlfriend had given me a love letter when we said goodbye and had a final kiss, and I read her letter again and again on the flight back to the UK, breaking my heart.

'I want to go back to Bahrain,' I cried to Mam. 'Why couldn't you have gone back to England on your own? How can you just take me out of school?'

'It'll work out,' Mam said. 'You'll soon settle back in.'

I was absolutely devastated, but no amount of begging and tears could have changed Mam's mind.

It was April 2001, we'd been in the Middle East for four years and I had just turned thirteen. Finally leaving Bahrain came as a massive shock at the end of an unsettling few months. Mam had been talking incessantly about her homesickness and how she needed to be around her old friends and everything that was familiar to her.

'Can't you talk her round?' I pleaded with Ronnie many times.

'We're trying to work it out,' he always said. 'I'm doing my best to convince your mum to stay, but you know how she is.'

Mam's state of mind rubbed off on everyone and made the atmosphere in the house super-tense.

'She's being selfish,' I said to Ronnie one day. 'We're all happy. Why do we all have to do what she wants? It's not fair!'

'Like I say, I'm doing my best, James.'

Ronnie was an honest and reliable man and I believed him, but then it seemed like something really bad happened between him and Mam. I think it was around the Millennium, when we all went to Disneyland Paris for New Year. We had a great family holiday, apparently – me, my sisters, Ronnie and Mam – but I can hardly remember a thing. I do know that something wasn't right. I don't think there were big arguments, more an undercurrent of unease. I was hypersensitive to any threat to my equilibrium, and I still am. There was tension between Mam and Ronnie, and I was scared of where that might lead.

After that it seemed Mam became more eager than ever to leave Bahrain, and before I knew it, the decision was made. We were closing down our life on the compound and packing our bags for Britain.

I was so upset and angry, and I didn't hold back.

'How am I going to adapt to life back in Middlesbrough?' I shouted at Mam. 'How the hell is that even possible?'

'You'll be fine . . .'

'Can we come back, when you've got over your homesickness? Can we?'

I wasn't getting a lot of clarity from her by this point. She didn't completely rule out a return until right towards the end, so I clung on to some hope for longer than I probably should have. When Mam finally told me that we were going back to Middlesbrough for good, with no plans to return to the Middle East, I cried uncontrollably. My heart was so heavy I felt like I was being crushed really hard, right in the chest. The lack of control over my heart, my body and my whole life scared me. I felt like I had absolutely no power over anything that was happening to me, and it was terrifying.

'Are we genuinely doing this? Please can you stop this from happening? You're ruining my life!'

I was so emotional, begging Mam to change her mind but coming up against a brick wall. I sobbed into my pillow.

*She said she wished she never had me. Why can't she leave me here? She can get her wish. She can get rid of me.*

It sounds so dramatic now, but that was how it was for me. This really was the end of my world and my thoughts were that dark. I was in purgatory waiting to find out just how hellish my existence was about to become.

When one of the teachers at my school heard I was returning to my home town she looked at me warily and said with trepidation, 'But it's so rough back home, back where you're from.'

*Tell me about it. It's horrible. People are ruthless and violent and they swear and fight and rip the piss out of each other. I'll get bullied at school like there's no tomorrow. How am I going to survive? I'm so afraid, and I don't understand why my mam is putting me through this.*

I was going to join Rye Hills in Redcar, the local mixed comprehensive. It was a terrifying prospect. I'd heard that new kids had their heads flushed down the toilet on the first day. I would be joining part-way through Year 8, so it couldn't be worse. All the other kids would have been there since the start of Year 7, and they would all have their friends and their groups and their cliques. Nobody would want to befriend the strange kid with a turned-in eye who'd been living in Bahrain and didn't speak like them.

It was so unfair. I'd just started to feel like less of an outcast in Bahrain, and on the flight to England I could already feel myself sliding backwards. I'd be the odd one out again. I wouldn't fit in and I'd be picked on and bullied. I was very pissed off and full of apprehension.

I blinked as I opened my eyes and reached for my glasses. I was waking up in our old house in Winchester Road. I blinked and blinked again. It was real, this had actually happened.

Mam and Ronnie had kept our old house and rented it out while we were away. It was like the clocks had been turned back four years, except now the girls had the bedrooms and I had to sleep on the couch because there was no room for me upstairs.

It felt so unreal to wake up back in this house. I looked out of the back window at the tatty washing line in the garden and stared, wondering why and how all of this had happened. It was raining and overcast. I wanted to look at sun-drenched palm trees. I want to see Amira. I wanted to play football with my mates on the compound.

Not long after we came back Dad had a lot of his family down from Glasgow for Easter, and he took me and Sian out for the afternoon. I was really happy to have Dad back in my life – we picked things up again very easily – but I was also on edge about Mam complaining and losing the plot about our visits again. Mam still lived in the past when it came to my dad and had not mellowed one bit, but actually I don't remember the scenes being as bad as they used to be. I think it was probably because me and Sian were older now and could take ourselves off, or maybe Mam had too many other problems on her mind now and simply didn't have the mental energy.

I was with Dad, walking past a pub in Redcar, when I saw a sign advertising a kids' karaoke competition. The prize was £5 and an Easter egg, which caught my attention straight away.

'I could win that, Dad,' I said.

'I bet you could, son.'

He took me and Sian and a big crowd of Scottish relatives

down there later. Loads of kids had a turn, and then I got up and sang Bryan Adams' '(Everything I Do) I Do It For You'.

'You could hear a pin drop,' Dad recalls. 'Everybody in the pub stopped talking and all the family from Glasgow were crying like babies.'

I was buzzing, and the feeling took me back to being on the stage in Bahrain, when I sang the modern Major-General song. I won the fiver and the egg and sang another song – 'Amazed' by Lonestar.

Dad told me I was totally brilliant and my talent shone through. It meant a lot and I was so happy and proud of myself, but moments like that were rare. I didn't see a great deal of my dad, and opportunities to get up on stage were limited now I was out of my private school and the drama lessons I loved so much.

'Oi, posh boy!'

I was being taunted on my first day at Rye Hills, which was no surprise, although the chosen insult was something I could never have predicted. I wanted to laugh out loud. Me, a posh boy? This was brutal.

'So you lived in the desert did ya, posh boy? Or should we call you *Bahrain* boy?'

I decided pretty early on that I'd be cocky, to show the boys I could hold my own.

'OK, cool. You're really smart, comin' up with that . . .'

I think I gained a bit of respect for coming back with a retort of any kind rather than crumbling or just staying quiet. I certainly saved myself from getting my head flushed down the toilet, because that never happened.

I picked up the Middlesbrough accent again pretty quickly, because the smoothed-out accent I'd developed in Bahrain, where hardly any of my friends spoke with a regional accent, clearly wasn't going to do me any favours.

I also sussed out that if I gave the teachers a bit of cheek I gained not just a grudging respect from the other kids, but kudos too.

'Would you like to go and see the head teacher?' I was asked in one class, when I was playing up and not doing the work I had been asked to do.

'No it's OK, thanks, I've already met him.'

The lads who were the same age as me thought this kind of backchat was cool and gradually began to accept me, but nevertheless I still got bullied by the kids in the year above me.

'There's that freak who came from the desert,' they would say. 'Oi, desert boy! Or should we say Arthur-itis?'

They were taking the mickey out of my name, calling me 'James Arthur-itis' instead of the name I still went by – James Arthur-Rafferty.

'You can call me Raff,' I said to my classmates, as I liked the nickname I'd been given in Bahrain and thankfully that stuck instead.

'Oi, Raff! What was it like hangin' out with all them Pakis and dirty Arabs?' a lad shouted across the corridor one day.

I was speechless at that. I'd been shocked to hear those words even before I'd lived in Bahrain and made friends with Pakistanis and Arabs and people from so many different races and cultures. It was outrageous and it really angered me. So many kids in Redcar had inherited this small-minded, racist mentality. It wasn't their fault, it was all they knew, and I felt thankful that I'd had the opportunity to broaden my horizons.

A few months after we got back we moved into a bigger house on the Coast Road. Ronnie sorted this house out for us, even though at that point he and my mam were no longer the loved-up couple they once were. Their relationship was in trouble, and I was hearing whispers about them splitting up. I think they were on and off for quite a while – maybe a year – though at the time I was never really sure if Ronnie was away on business or staying away through choice, because nobody told me what was going on. Either way, he definitely wasn't there for us like he used to be. Mam wasn't there either, at least not emotionally, because the problems she had with Ronnie were really dragging her down and she was moody and disconnected.

Then everything went bang and fell apart, seemingly over-night. The plug was pulled on Coast Road and suddenly me, Mam and my three sisters were moving back into Winchester Road, this time without Ronnie. It was a time of confusion and turmoil and I was incredibly anxious, every waking moment. I couldn't believe we were back in our old house again and I didn't understand what had happened and couldn't ask. Mam was all over the place and Sian was turning into a Goth and cutting herself off from me. Nobody who mattered was talking to me and I was short-tempered and very angry.

I really missed Ronnie being around every day. I was four-teen now. He'd been in my life for eleven years and had become a real role model to me. It was hard being in a house full of females and I felt very isolated and lonely. I had no choice but to resign myself to the fact we'd probably end up in a situa-tion a bit like the one I had with my dad, seeing Ronnie randomly at weekends, and probably with a lot of shouting from Mam to send us on our way. I guessed he'd have to sort out some kind of proper custody arrangement with Jazz and Neve, because they were his daughters, and I dreaded all the drama I imagined a court case might create.

Nothing turned out how I imagined. I didn't see Ronnie again for months, and when I asked Mam what the hell was going on she didn't give me straight answers. She implied that Ronnie had let her down and broken her trust, but I also heard that he accused her of doing something wrong, something that showed him that she wasn't the person he thought she was. In many ways it was like a repeat of what I knew of Mam and Dad's break-up: a shit storm of recriminations, bitterness and anger, all culminating in Mam being left on her own with the kids. Except now she had four kids and Neve was the one still in nappies, just as I had been when Mam and Dad split up.

One night I went into the local rugby club to watch a Middlesbrough game on Sky. I was so scared going into the club because I wasn't a rugby lad and felt like an outsider. I sat in the corner biting my nails and avoiding eye contact with the lads who were playing pool, because I didn't want them to say, 'Who the hell are you?'

After the game, I got up to leave as quickly as I could and I spotted Ronnie across the room. I hadn't seen him for months on end and I didn't know what to do or say. I was too anxious to talk to him, and so I walked past him, straight out of the club.

Afterwards he came around to see me.

'Why did you blank me?' he asked. 'What the hell has your mother said?'

I told him she'd claimed he cheated on her, which is what she had eventually told me.

'It's not the case,' he said angrily. 'Your mam did something to me . . . I just can't be with her any more.'

*What more can go wrong? Life is so confusing. Why is this happening?*

After that Ronnie disappeared off the face of the earth. I can remember there was a lot of inquisition over whether he might appear again.

'He doesn't want anything to do with any of you,' Mam said one time. 'It's over. Forget about Ronnie. You'll never see him again.'

It was harsh and Mam was not in her right mind when she said that, but unbelievably she was right. I never did see Ronnie again, not ever. It really was like aliens had come and taken him to another planet, because he vanished without trace.

I was baffled and so upset. Ronnie was a really good guy and disappearing is such an extreme thing to do, for anyone. He had brought me and Sian up from the ages of three and four and had been a great stepdad to us. How could he just walk away and never see us again? Even more incomprehensible was the fact he left Jasmin and Neve. They were his own flesh and blood, and he absolutely adored them. Jasmin had always been his little bumblebee, the girl who could wrap him round her little finger and melt his heart. How could he leave Jazz? He loved both of his daughters, and I know he cared a lot for Sian and me. It was so confusing why he'd done this to us.

*Is it me? What have I done wrong? Why does nobody want me?*

I thought about my dad, and how he'd fought so hard to keep in contact with Sian and me, regardless of all the trauma he went through with Mam. He did it because he loved us.

That's what parents do. They fight tooth and nail for their kids, whatever the obstacles in their way. They go to court and have custody battles, because that's how much it matters.

'What the hell's happened, Mam? This doesn't make any sense. Surely he'll come back? Nobody can just disappear, can they?'

I didn't ever get any sense out of Mam when I tried to find answers, and to this day I am still very confused about Ronnie. I hoped he might have got in contact when I was on *The X Factor* and I've tried to find him many times, without success. I heard, while writing this book, that Ronnie once said he was cutting himself off because he didn't want Mam to use Jazz and Neve against him for the rest of his life in the way she used me and Sian against Dad. That's the closest I've come to any explanation.

Mam's behaviour was wild and extreme. She became very irrational and was shouting a lot and relaying what had happened in the most dramatic way to her friends. There were always people coming around to comfort her, and I'd watch all this chaos unfolding night after night and just want to escape.

Any chance we could, me and Sian would sit in front of Cartoon Network or Nickelodeon, just to try to switch off from the madness for a while. Sian had a boyfriend who she was spending a lot of time with. We were nowhere near as close as we were when we were younger, so there were lots of times when I was on my own. I'd slope off on my own to play *Pro Evolution Soccer* for hours, just to escape and forget about all the shit that had happened, and how much we had lost.

The foundations of my life had gone, that's how it felt. I was very afraid of what was going to happen next and most of all I felt incredibly lonely.

# CHAPTER TWELVE

*Wow. This is wild. Is this my life now?*

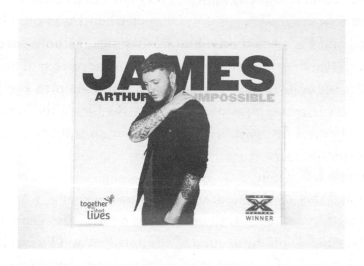

'Could somebody give that child a wee shake, because it would be really nice to talk to him after the break.'

It was the morning after I won *The X Factor* and I was waiting to be interviewed by Lorraine, live on ITV. I was so tired and out of it I was sleeping right up until the last minute, and Lorraine burst out laughing when the camera panned round and she spotted me, out for the count under a coat on a sofa.

*That child.*

I felt exactly like a little boy.

I didn't have a clue what was happening to me and I had no control over my life. Overnight I had a management team and now I was completely dependent on them. It was as if they'd become my parents.

'Where do I live now?' I asked my new manager, Caroline. 'Do I have to stay in London?'

I'd been wondering if I'd have to go back to sleeping on Dawson's sofa, because I'd be homeless again after moving out of the *X Factor* hotel.

'Yes, you need to be in London. We've got you a flat in Kensal Rise.'

I'd never been there, but apparently, it was in north London. At least I had somewhere to live, but what was it going to be like, living on my own in a part of London I didn't know at all, six hours away from all my friends and family?

'Do I have money?'

I felt like I was asking for my dinner money for primary school.

'Yes. You've got money. It's all organised. You've got money, you've got the flat and we'll be going around the country on a tour, signing singles and that kind of thing.'

'OK,' I said flatly. 'That's good.'

For the whole of winner's week, I'd be doing 'promo' and 'PAs', which meant publicity and personal appearances. I just nodded and accepted what I was being told. I would also end up with about £800,000 in the bank once I received the money from Syco for my new recording contract. Almost every label within Sony had pitched for me and I didn't have to sign with Syco but I did, as I believed they had a good vision for me and would help me achieve my ambitions. I even took a phone call from Simon Cowell.

'Thank you for saving my show,' he said.

*Wow. This is wild. Is this my life now?*

I was scared to death and couldn't take it in at all.

The management team was made up of nice people, but they were all very posh-sounding and 'London' and I couldn't identify with them. I wished I had my mates or my sisters around me, anyone who understood me and could empathise with me or at least talk to me on my level about all this stuff. I knew I could pick the phone up to any of them, but I felt like I was in another world now, one that was completely disconnected from life in Middlesbrough.

During *The X Factor* I'd had a few awkward conversations, when I'd called one of my friends to share the excitement of an event.

'Man, you'll never guess what. We're all going on the red carpet, for the premiere of *Skyfall*. Daniel Craig will be there!'

To me showbiz stuff like that was pretty meaningless without having someone to share it with. That's why I phoned my old friends, but it always felt wrong. Half the time I'd catch someone when they were coming off a twelve-hour shift in a call centre, and even though my mates were always very supportive and pleased for me, I was paranoid they thought I was bragging.

I called my friends less and less, and I never told them or anybody else how scared I was feeling now I'd won the competition and was starting this new life on my own. I wanted to act all independent and to seem like I could cope. I was nearly twenty-five. I felt I had to do this thing all by myself. I was a solo artist and all my *X Factor* family had dispersed. I didn't even have anybody to just hang out with in London, and I had no other option but to get on with it. This was my life now. It was just me, alone and worried, wondering what the hell was going to happen. Every time I did events it felt like they weren't really happening, because there was no one to witness it, at least not anybody I really cared about.

When I moved into my new flat I felt jittery, right from the start. From the moment I turned the key in the door my heart was racing. I looked around and tried to take in what was happening to me. The flat was smart and well furnished – a million times better than my old bedsit – but I didn't feel any excitement or pleasure from being in this new situation.

Even though this was a much homelier environment than being in the fancy hotel during *The X Factor*, I felt instantly less at ease in the flat. I guess I knew the hotel was a temporary set-up, and I had all the other contestants and hustle and bustle around me. Ultimately that wasn't my life, but this was. It felt so odd, like I'd stolen someone's life and should not have been there, because nothing in the flat was mine, and nothing was familiar. Even the sounds and smells of the place were unsettling. There were train tracks at the back and when I opened the window I could smell London streets and pollution. I'd have done anything to be by the sea, on the coast; in a heartbeat, I'd have gone back to my old bedsit on the seafront at Saltburn.

The fact was, I simply didn't know how to live here. It wasn't just the flat, it was my whole lifestyle. Management was constantly calling me up and telling me there would be a car coming to take me to this photo shoot or that interview. It should have been so exciting and I should have been lapping it all up, reaping the rewards for all my hard work.

Instead I wished I could go to bed and not answer the door, because I just couldn't cope with it.

I was still on the combination of pills I'd been prescribed during the show and they weren't helping. I was tired all the time and it felt like my nerve endings had been burnt away, suppressing my emotions. I was never fully with it and I was just going through the motions with management like a bit of a puppet, doing what I was told by these strangers who were now controlling my life.

During interviews, I found it odd talking about myself all the time, saying the same things over and over again. It felt narcissistic and that unsettled me because I wasn't that person. Journalists were telling me I was the most famous man in Britain and people wanted to know everything about me. The truth was *I* didn't know everything about me. I had no idea who I was.

*You're lost. You don't know who you are and you need to find yourself, fast. If you don't you're going to fall through the cracks.*

I couldn't find myself; I was a million miles off the right track and I didn't know where to even start to look. I functioned OK when I was busy doing what I was told, because then I didn't have time to fret or panic. There was so much to do in the aftermath of the show it was crazy. The publicity was never-ending. There was my record deal and first album to discuss, as well as the upcoming tours – first the X *Factor* tour in January, then my own European tour at the start of 2014.

I had a sharp chest pain in the flat one night. My breathing wasn't right at all. I was starting to panic, thinking something was wrong with my heart.

*It's OK, James, take deep breaths. It's an anxiety attack. You can breathe through it.*

I didn't listen to my voice of reason. The voice of fear was much louder, booming all around my head.

*You can't breathe! You're struggling for air. You're going to have a heart attack! This is the one that's going to kill you. You're going to die, James.*

The terror of my situation was closing in on me. I was under so much pressure. I was not in control. I had no clue what to do except worry and panic.

*It's OK, James, take deep breaths.*

I opened the window. The cold air hit me and I managed to keep breathing, slowly regaining control. It took a full hour of me pacing around the room, but somehow, I managed to get through this panic attack without calling an ambulance. I was shaken up, but I'd survived. I was alive.

I had nothing to eat in the flat and eventually I had to go out to get some food. I started to worry about whether someone would tap me on the shoulder and ask if I was that guy who won *The X Factor*. Then I imagined myself turning around and saying, 'Oh, yes I am.'

*Shit! That is who I am now. How has that happened? I don't want to be that guy.*

I couldn't do it. Even though I was hungry and needed some food I couldn't go out. I had a conversation with myself.

*Go on, James, you'll be fine. There's a Nando's just at the top of the road. It's not far, it won't take long.*

*No way, I can't do it.*

*You can. You could put your hood up. Nobody would even notice you. You'll be in and out in no time.*

No *way, I can't do it. It's too hard. What if I have a panic attack in Nando's?*

While I talked to myself, in my own head, there were other voices, trying to drown out my conversation. The voices told me I was going to die. I should listen to them, because if I went to Nando's I would die for sure.

*See, I can't go to get food because I'm going to die.*

*How could you die, just going to the end of the road?*

*I could, I know I could. My heart's already thumping. It's going to get worse, it's going to explode.*

This conversation went on for about three hours. Eventually the voice of reason won, I think because I was so tired and hungry by that point. I really needed something to eat. I wouldn't die. I put on my hoodie and left the flat.

*Breathe. Breathe. Breathe. Hopefully it won't be busy. Hopefully I won't be in there for long. Hopefully the person on the till won't look me in the eye, and I won't have to look at them. I can't do that. I can't look at them, no way. I'd rather not bother.*

I got a few metres down the road and started struggling for breath.

*If you get through the door of Nando's everyone will take pictures of you. The anxiety will be too much. You won't be able to breathe. Your heart will burst and you will die on the floor. When you're dead on the floor everyone will take more pictures of you.*

I turned around and went back to the flat, rushing inside and slamming the front door behind me, trying to shut out my fear. I was breathing with less of a struggle now, but only just. The panic was subsiding, but very slowly.

Eventually I tried to sleep, to shut the world out completely.

I was exhausted and it was a relief to drift off, wrapped up in my bed, like a little boy, hidden from the world.

When I woke up the next day I remembered the craziest dream I'd had. In the dream, I'd won *The X Factor* and had this amazing new life at my feet. I had a new flat in London and a brand-new singing career ahead of me. In the dream, I was top of the charts with the fastest-selling single in *X Factor* history – a cover of Shontelle's 'Impossible'.

*Impossible.*

I could still glimpse the dream as I opened my eyes and blinked. It was falling out of focus now and slipping out of reach, like dreams do.

Then I blinked again, put on my glasses and looked around my unfamiliar bedroom.

*What is this place? Where the hell am I?*

That's when it dawned on me that I hadn't just had a dream, I was waking up *to* that dream. This was my reality.

I started panicking.

*What do I do, what do I do? Shit! I'll just close my eyes and go back to sleep. I don't want anything to do with this.*

It was so terrifying. I felt completely detached from reality. I wasn't in control of any aspect of my life but I was trapped in it. I felt fully mad, actually – one hundred per cent crazy, and that scared me to death. There was no way I was going to survive this.

I texted my sisters to see if they were OK, but I didn't tell them how I was feeling. I was supposed to be the successful brother now, the one who'd lived the rags-to-riches fairy tale and they could finally be proud of. No way could I tell them it was all a sham.

I pulled the covers back over my head and went back to

sleep, and when I woke up a few hours later I was shocked all over again that I was in this strange, scary place. I wanted to run like mad and get the hell out of there. The urge was so powerful I decided there was only one way I could stop it.

I did what I'd always done in the past when I wanted to escape: I got myself some weed and smoked a few joints, trying to forget my new life was real. I drifted into oblivion, and it was such a massive relief. I'd missed the feeling, and at last I'd found something I recognised again, something that could give me comfort and shield me from the sharp edges of reality.

# CHAPTER THIRTEEN

*You're not like the other kids. They don't like you really. They'll kick you out of the group*

The first thing I thought when I opened my eyes was, 'I hope Mam's having a bad day,' because if Mam was having a bad day she wouldn't get out of bed and I wouldn't have to go to school.

I tried my best to settle in, but I hated Rye Hills. There were fights all the time and all the kids would gather to watch, baying for blood. I never got involved in fights like that, but the older boys would push me around on a daily basis, blind-siding me, tripping me up or ramming me into doors. It was so demoralising and unsettling, and getting through each day was a nerve-racking ordeal.

Thankfully I never got properly beaten up, perhaps because I decked one of the tough kids quite early on. We had been doing PE on the field and this one particular lad would not let up, calling me names and going on about me coming from the desert and being bong-eyed. I tried to keep my head down and ignore him because I knew if I spoke, my accent would get me into more trouble, but he was in my ear the whole time as we walked off the field, winding me up relentlessly.

'Are you listenin' to me, posh boy?'

I was so sick and tired of these taunts and I snapped that day, turning around and punching the kid in the face with everything I had. He went down and was stumbling on the ground, unable to get back up.

'Wow, what the hell just happened?' the other kids said. 'Did Raff really just do that?'

Nobody could believe that the oddball kid had hit this hard nut, but I wasn't proud of myself: in fact, I was scared I'd get expelled. In the event the boy said nothing, because he was embarrassed and didn't want the teachers to know what had happened. The upshot was that I gained a lot of respect from the other kids my age, and a certain amount of protection from the older lads.

I eventually made friends with the skater kids in my year but I never felt I fully fitted in with the group, despite trying really hard. I'd go to the skate park and I saved up to get roller blades, but even when I was in the middle of the group I felt like an outsider.

*You're not like the other kids. They don't like you really. They'll kick you out of the group. You don't belong.*

I was constantly full of nerves and felt afraid to be myself. I didn't even know who the real me was, and I always felt like I was playing a version of myself, a version I hoped would be OK and would let me get by in the group. I didn't ever feel connected to the other boys or to people in general; there was a definite disconnect between me and the whole world, because I just wasn't like everybody else.

My home life wasn't normal in any way. Mam had spiralled out of all control since Ronnie disappeared and I dreaded going home after school because I was so desperately unhappy with everything that was going on. We were batshit poor, living on welfare, and it seemed all anyone could talk about was money, or the lack of it. It was back to Smiley Faces for tea and we started to get bailiffs at the door and eviction notices landing all the time.

I didn't care that I didn't have the latest Adidas Poppers like my mates, but I did care about the knocks at the door. They shook me, because I had no control over them and I felt constantly under threat and on my guard, watching and wondering what was going to happen next.

'I've been left with four kids,' Mam would wail. 'How am I supposed to deal with this?'

Mam was forever going on about how she'd been let down by my dad and by Ronnie. It had been bad enough when she used to moan about how Dad had left her with two kids. Now she'd been left with four kids, and her bitterness and regret and anger had not just doubled, it was completely off the scale.

'It's not fair, I'm on my own!' was something Mam said often. I felt exactly the same way. I was all alone in the world, and I was rudderless. Ronnie was gone, and to all intents and purposes Mam had gone. She was not herself mentally, and she was not there for me on any level. I didn't recognise then that she was suffering from severe depression. I understand her actions now and I forgive her for what unfolded, but at the time I was a very angry and confused young lad.

'Get up, James! Why aren't you at school?'

Mam was screaming like a banshee. It was 11 a.m. and she had only just got up. Some days she never got up at all, and I always prayed that it would be one of those days, so I wouldn't have to go to school.

'I'm sick,' I'd say as I lay on the couch in the living room with my duvet wrapped around me.

'No, you're not. Get your uniform on and get out the house, now!'

I'd fight and argue, because I really didn't want to go to school and I was annoyed with Mam for letting our lives become so dysfunctional. There was no routine and no discipline. I didn't have a proper bed. Jasmin was missing a lot of school, and Neve, who was still a toddler, was not getting the attention she needed.

'Why didn't *you* get up? What about Jasmin? Why the hell isn't *she* at school?'

'James, why is it that all I ever get is the worst word in your mouth?'

We'd have a full-scale screaming match which inevitably ended in Mam telling me I was just like my dad, that I was so aggressive and angry and she wished she'd never given birth to me. That was still her killer line, every time. Then she'd push me out the door to school.

I got a reputation for being late, or not turning up at all. I'd get detentions and suspensions because I wasn't doing the work, I was angry in the classroom and I was truanting. I had no respect for authority and I can remember when the World Cup qualifiers were on TV I'd just kick the door of the school open and walk home to watch the games. The only classes I liked were English and music. The English teacher, Mr Stockwell, was really encouraging and gave me a lot of praise for my creative writing, and I was fascinated by the music teacher because he played the guitar. I didn't take music for GCSE though, so that didn't last long. I thought I was too good for music classes and my mates weren't doing it, so I reckoned it would be a load of shit and gave it up.

It wasn't long before I was on the radar with Social Services, with questions being asked about whether I needed a social worker for support. The school assigned me a counsellor, a fantastic lady called Celia. I'd pour my heart out to her and she'd talk to me and explain why I might be feeling a certain way. I'd leave the sessions feeling great. I remember it so vividly: to have a professional like her making a correlation between how I was feeling and what had happened to me was so helpful, but for some reason it didn't last.

Sian was coping so much better than me. She usually got herself together and went to school. She kept her head down and didn't argue with Mam the way I did. She also played really good rock and pop-punk music; in my eyes Sian was sorted and cool.

'What's that?' I'd ask, playing air guitar as I listened to her music.

'Shut up,' she'd snap back, making me feel like the annoying little brother. 'Just go away, will ya?'

The closeness we'd had when we were younger had been eroded, and Sian became quite cold and confrontational with me. I wanted my big sister to be my ally in my battles with Mam, but Sian went the other way, either distancing herself from me or getting really annoyed with me when I argued with Mam. As the situation at home steadily declined Sian took Mam's side come what may, even when Mam was exaggerating or plainly lying about my behaviour. This drove a massive wedge between us.

I know now that Sian had decided it was safer to fall out with me than with Mam. It was anything to keep the peace with Mam, because life was hard enough as it was. Sian was just protecting herself from trauma as much as she could, but I didn't understand that back then. The way Mam treated me already made me feel like a bad person, and seeing Sian siding with her fuelled those feelings.

*You're not normal, James. You're angry. You're bad. You're the misfit of the family.*

Every week, every day, seemed to bring a new low.

Mam started to go missing for three or four days at a time, off on benders, partying with her mates. Me and Sian would be in complete disarray, worrying ourselves sick about where she was and what state she was in. Between us we tried to look after Jasmin and Neve as best we could, but even though we were both trying to do the right thing together, me and Sian would still be at loggerheads with each other. Sian stepped into the mother role, and she started telling me what to do, which I didn't like one bit. By the time Mam came home we'd both be at each other's throats, and at breaking point.

'Where the hell have you been, Mam?'

'Oh, just out with my friend, James.'

'Just out with your friend? You can't do that Mam. You've

got four kids! You've got two little girls. Neve is a toddler and Jasmin is seven years old. What the hell are you doing?'

'Don't you dare speak to me like that. I'm a single mum and I need to have a break and go out sometimes. You don't understand anything, James. Tell him, Sian!'

Sian would tell me to stop shouting and kicking off. She didn't support Mam's excuses, but when Mam said I was being too angry and aggressive, Sian always agreed with her, just to calm things down.

Sometimes I phoned my dad and told him what was going on.

'Aye, son, that's what your mam's like.'

*Brilliant*.

I learned that Mam had behaved that way when they were together – going out on benders – but the fact Dad was never surprised by anything I told him was no help or comfort. He was still married to Jackie – still is – and, rightly or wrongly, I always got the impression he was afraid to rock the boat or do anything that might upset his marriage. He had my sister Charlotte to consider, and getting involved in our mess was the last thing he wanted.

On Sian's sixteenth birthday we called the police because Mam had been missing for days and days on end and we were really worried. Tellingly, neither of us can remember any details, other than that we took turns skipping school to look after Jasmin and Neve. 'I've blocked it out,' Sian has told me. 'I'm the same,' I said. 'It was such a shitty time I never wanted to remember any of it.'

Mam started to bring men friends back to the house. I didn't really like any of them but some I hated, because they told me what to do.

'You'll be gone next week! Don't tell me what to do. This is my house, not yours.'

I had full-on fist fights with a couple of them, and no matter how rude or bossy the men had been with me, Mam always blamed me for causing the trouble, every time.

*What is my life? Why is Mam blaming me? Why does she put these strangers before me? Am I not worth anything to her? Am I a worthless piece of shit?*

On the eve of Sian's English GCSE Mam was blasting out Madonna downstairs while she entertained her latest man friend. Sian was trying to sleep and she had to go downstairs and ask Mam to turn the music down.

'Who's the teenager?' I said, baffled and angry. 'Why is Mam behaving like this?'

Mam was only nineteen when she had Sian and it seemed she was trying to recapture her youth and have some fun after going through two divorces. Mental illness wasn't something I recognised. I knew nothing about depression and therefore had no understanding of why Mam was behaving this way.

On another occasion, Sian got a text at school, from one of Mam's best friends, asking her to come home quick. Somehow Sian got out of school and ran home to find Mam passed out on the sofa and Neve toddling round in a nappy. Sian recalls it as the worst day of her life. 'What the actual fuck am I meant to do?' she thought as she stood in the living room, feeling her world falling apart around her.

I think it was at this point, after the passing out episode, that Mam did start to discuss her depression with us. She told us for the first time she had borderline personality disorder, and when I thought about her extreme behaviour this fitted, although my understanding of any kind of depression was very limited. What I could see was that Mam was either on a crazy high, partying like there was no tomorrow, or she was in the pits of the blackest despair and saying some frightening, terrible things.

There were many times when Mam threatened to walk into the sea and drown herself. Once, when Jazz refused to speak to her, Mam lied that she had breast cancer, just to get Jazz to talk to her again. That shows how mentally ill she was, because if she was in her right mind she would never have done such a cruel thing. Mam was having a major breakdown, basically, and was falling completely off the rails.

It was such a lonely time for us kids. Even though Sian and I had very different methods of dealing with Mam we were both at war with her. I was verbalising my hurt and anger while Sian was trying to contain hers, but the pain and anxiety was there for each of us. We were trying to hold it together because Mam wasn't, but we were going off the rails just like her, because we were way too young to deal with this level of pressure and fear and responsibility.

Sian withdrew and I exploded. I punched walls when I felt my anger boil over, because if I didn't do that I was afraid I was going to hit someone. My knuckles would be black and blue and bleeding, but I hit the walls time and time again. This wasn't enough. I trashed things and got into scraps with other boys. My nose got busted in one of them, but I didn't care. There was so much anger inside me, and I had to get it out.

All Sian and I both wanted was to be happy, or at least as happy as we had been in Bahrain. Any level of happiness would have been better than what we had, but it didn't seem attainable at all.

'Why can't you sort yourself out, Mam? Why are we living like this?'

Whenever I confronted Mam she totally flipped and went off on a rant, berating me and telling me yet again I was just like my dad. I was angry, I was aggressive. I was nothing but a nuisance to her, an encumbrance she wished she didn't have to put up with.

'One hundred per cent I wish I'd had you aborted,' she screamed one night. 'Get out of my house!'

'Aw, Mam. Not this again. No way.'

'I mean it. Get out and don't come back.'

'Are you serious? Where am I going to go?'

'Go to your mates. I don't care. Go wherever the hell you like. But you're not staying here.'

She threw me out the back door, just like she had when I was eight years old and we had the row about my season ticket going missing. The difference was, this time she had no intention of letting me back in. She made that very clear. The door was locked behind me and I was out in the cold in the clothes I stood up in.

I was fourteen years old, miserable to the core and terrified.

# CHAPTER FOURTEEN

*Come on! I want my mind back.*
*What does this all mean?*

'Has James Arthur put on a few X-tra pounds?'

I was looking at the headline in the *Sun* and wanted to die with shame.

I was on the *X Factor* tour and I looked like a whale. There had been about six weeks between the end of the show and the start of the tour, and when I wasn't being chaperoned to events by my management I spent the time destroying myself with junk food and drugs.

I lived on Burger King for breakfast, KFC for lunch and Subway and Domino's pizzas for supper. Domino's was my favourite, because I could have it delivered to my flat and didn't have to face the ordeal of going outside and feeling panic-stricken about having a heart attack on the street or being photographed dead on the pavement. Having said that, I still found it hard just to greet the delivery guy at the door. I wished I could just grab my pizza without having to look at anyone, and I'd never, ever look the guy in the eye when I gave him the money.

*It's OK now. You can eat the pizza. You don't need to panic.*

One night I started to have a panic attack before I could eat the pizza, because of the stress of opening the door to the delivery guy. I thought he was judging me.

*Are you that guy who won* The X Factor? *You look like a bag head, man. Look at the state of you. You're ugly. Urgh, I don't want to look at you because you're so disgusting.*

I lost it when I heard that chatter in my head. My breathing got more and more shallow and my heartbeat was erratic, off the scale, out of all control. It felt like I was being repeatedly thumped with a hard fist from inside my body. I was not going to survive this. My heart was punching itself out of my chest and I had to get to hospital. If I didn't I would definitely die of a heart attack tonight, alone in my flat.

*I'm not getting through this. I'm not ready to die, not yet. Hello? Can you hear me?*

'Which service do you require?'

'Ambulance. I need an ambulance fast. I'm having a heart attack. Come quick. I'm dying here . . . shit, I don't want to die.'

127

I paced the room, gasping for air in the silence, waiting for the siren. As soon as I heard the ambulance outside I began to feel a little bit better. Help was coming, but my breathing was still out of control. When the paramedic checked me over I was sweating and trembling, telling him to save my life because I really was not ready to die.

My blood pressure was fine. Physically there was nothing wrong. It was just another anxiety attack and it wasn't going to kill me after all. I had to take deep breaths. I needed to try to stay calm and keep breathing as steadily as I could. The paramedic assured me it was a mental thing, not a physical one.

*Mental? That's worse. How the hell do you fix a mental thing? Am I having a major mental breakdown, like Mam did?*

I started having panic attacks on a nightly basis, and often it was something as innocuous as the sound of a train passing behind the flat that set me off, making me catch my breath and feel instantly scared. The noise would clatter around my head, and then I'd hear screaming and voices.

*You're going to die. You're going to have a heart attack. This is the one that is going to kill you.*

I lost count of the number of times I called out an ambulance to that flat. I felt so stupid, because no matter how many times a paramedic reassured me it was a panic attack and there was nothing physically wrong with my heart, I was always convinced each and every time that this was different, *this* was the killer attack. It was exactly what had happened backstage at *The X Factor*. There is no way I'd have created all the drama of calling an ambulance to the studios if I didn't think I was going to die. Being checked over by a professional instantly made me feel better, and that had become part of my recurring problem now. I got it in my head that I had to call an ambulance and I had to have a paramedic check me over because reassurance from a medical professional was the only thing that ever put my mind at rest when I got in that state. Only then could I start breathing more easily.

My management must have been aware that I had issues because they were impossible to ignore. Sometimes I had to ask Caroline to stop the car so I could get out and breathe and when we started to fly to places, the security gate at the airport always triggered me.

'Do you mind if you go through and I'll follow you? I just need to sit down for a minute.'

'Of course.'

I didn't go into any detail with my management and I kept my dark thoughts to myself. I was worried that if I told anyone what I was thinking – that if I went through security I would instantly drop dead on the other side – they would think I was a crazy person.

*Look through the gate, James. There is your dead body on the floor. That's you. This is the end.*

I'd have a clear vision of my corpse. It was so terrifying and I had to have some very long and scary conversations with myself, desperately trying to convince myself the image wasn't real. My head would be ready to explode when I eventually got on the plane, trembling with nerves and feeling so stupid and frail.

I was smoking a lot of weed too, every night. It was something I promised myself I could do again, when I came out the other side of *The X Factor*. I couldn't smoke it during the process but there were so many times when I thought, 'Just get through this and you can have the biggest bag of weed ever.' Now that I was free to do what I wanted most of the time I just let myself go, completely, and I started smoking myself into oblivion every night.

I knew my behaviour was dangerous, but after all the pressure I'd been under on the show I'd kind of given up, because I was just too tired to care. All I wanted to do was switch myself off and forget about all the worries and fears that preyed on my mind. The only time I was anything like happy was when I was high, and so that's how I wanted to be; baked on marijuana, eating junk food.

I started bingeing on sex too. Ever since I'd been in the spotlight women had been giving me their phone numbers and contacting me through social media. Even journalists would try to give me their details when they did interviews for the show. I'd developed a bit of a reputation in the press as a 'player' and a 'ladies' man', which was fuelled by the way I flirted with Caroline Flack and a few stories that had ended up in the papers, about me partying with pretty girls in nightclubs and stuff like that.

I liked the female attention I was getting and I got a kick out of girls flirting with me sexually. In hindsight, I can see I was looking for validation. Having hot women interested in me boosted my self-confidence and made me feel less ugly and disgusted with my body. I was incredibly insecure about myself as a human being and sex became like another drug to me; one that could help me slay my self-doubts and self-loathing.

The one thing that didn't change after *The X Factor* was my belief in my music. Whatever state I was in and however low or messed up I felt, I had a massive amount of confidence in my ability as a performer. The only time I ever felt anything like normal was when I was singing and playing the guitar. I wish that had been enough to save me from myself, but it wasn't. I had too many demons and too much self-doubt about every other aspect of my life, and that's why I grabbed at anything I thought would free me from my fears and anxieties.

Rita Ora gave me a massive confidence boost in those early months. After I won the show she started texting and ringing me, which blew my mind. The first time she called I just couldn't compute it at all. Everything in my life felt crazy and I was so puzzled that someone like Rita was actually interested in me.

'I can't even take this right now,' I told her. 'This is too weird.'

I genuinely wondered what she wanted and couldn't work it out. She is so beautiful and such a strong alpha female and I told myself this couldn't be real.

*Rita's made a mistake. She must think I'm someone cool, someone I'm not. This is so confusing.*

Rita didn't give up, even though sometimes when she rang me I was too afraid to even answer my phone. We eventually met up during the *X Factor* tour, when we found ourselves in the same town. I was on a high that night, after coming off stage. Performing live always gives me the best buzz in the world and I had a lot to be happy about. 'Impossible' had been nominated for a Brit award and I had this beautiful, amazing woman pursuing me. However nervous I was about meeting Rita, I recognised this was the stuff fairy tales are made of, and I wanted to go into that world.

We had a few drinks and I went onto her tour bus. There was a lot of magic there and it was an amazing night. Rita seemed really, really into me, but I still couldn't quite believe it. I thought maybe she was a girl who was a bit like me – someone from a working-class background who found fame and a mad life and was a little bit lost. I also wondered if she was just a very good actress, playing with me. I was very stoned that night and my paranoia was sky-high the next day. What if this was all some elaborate hoax?

Me and Rita met up a few more times after that and had some more amazing nights. I don't know what my performance was like on the few occasions we had sex because I was always stoned, but I can't have been that bad. Rita wanted to see me again; this was crazy.

'I'm in love with you,' she told me one night.

She said it so sincerely I wanted to believe her, even though it seemed insane and I had a voice in my mind all the time saying, 'Rita's such a catch. Is she messin' with you?' Rita repeated the same words several times after that and she sounded so believable every time. 'I'm in love with you, James.' I hadn't misheard and my heart was beating wildly. This was real, but even so I still felt I was in a weird fantasy bubble that was going to pop at any moment.

I started to tell Rita I was in love with her too. I felt like I was – I think I was – but I still couldn't get my head around what was happening.

Friends and family would say to me, 'Wow, what's it like to be living the dream?'

I didn't have an answer, because when I was back in my own reality – in my flat, with nobody to share my life with – I was so, so lonely. I craved normality and so many times I wanted to tell my sisters and my friends what I really thought: 'I want so badly to go back to being in my old bedsit with absolutely nothing to worry about. I was better off when I was dreaming about this life rather than living it.'

I couldn't say it. I should have told the truth and shared my burden with the people who really love me, but I never did.

One night I had the biggest panic attack ever in my flat. The train running past triggered it, and I was so scared. My lungs wouldn't work properly and I couldn't breathe, and voices started screaming in my head really loudly. It was terrifying. I thought I was not just having a heart attack this time, my brain was going to explode out of my head.

I desperately wanted to take a complete breath, but every time I tried to inhale I took in less and less air. I ran to the bathroom and started splashing cold water on my face, trying to shock myself back to reality.

*Come on! I want my mind back. What does this all mean? Why am I here?*

For a short time, I thought Rita was the reason I was here. She was what it was all about. I guess I became a little bit obsessed with her, and now it was me calling her. It was wild — and there were so many wild things going on in my life, all the time.

I started working on my first album and to celebrate I got a massive tattoo of King Arthur on my right wrist and hand, so almost my whole arm was tattooed, right down to my knuckles. It was so ugly and narcissistic — it looked more like a glove than a sleeve — but at the time I loved it and told interviewers I had it done because I felt like a king. I'd first started having tattoos when I was about nineteen, when I let my friend practise on my left arm with his gun. Nothing ever came out looking how it should and he ruined my upper arm, so I had lots of cover-up work done afterwards. Now both my arms were full of tattoos. I thought I looked good, and I guess I was making a statement: I wasn't an *X Factor* product. The show was over, I was in charge of my image and I was living my life the way I wanted to.

Of course, inside I didn't feel like a king or even that I had any control over my life. The *X Factor* tour was a big success up and down the country, but it's a blur in my memory, because I was so stoned and drugged up on all my anti-depressants every time I went on stage. I was struggling for survival every day and I didn't even feel like myself. Under my skin, I was still the same frightened, fearful little boy I'd always been.

It didn't help that, out of nowhere as far as I was concerned, Rita went cold on me. I saw pictures of her with other guys in the press and I was devastated. I should have just given up the ghost, but I was confused and I tried to reconnect with her. By this time, we'd been having our thing on and off for a few months, and I was heartbroken she just seemed to disappear. It hit me really hard, and I needed more valida-tion that ever.

If I'm honest, I became a bit of a slag after Rita. I was chat-ting to hundreds of women online or on WhatsApp after swapping numbers with them via Twitter, and I started to sleep with so many of them I lost count. Sometimes I'd have one girl coming to the flat in the daytime and another at night, then a different one the next morning. They were usually the same type: babe station girls, or glamour models who appeared in magazines like *Nuts*. If I saw someone I fancied I'd contact her on social media and tell her blatantly I wanted to have sex. It was ridiculously easy. The girls would come to my flat, have sex and leave. Looking back, I think I chose those types of girls because I thought there would be no emotional attachment and it would be just pure sex, and with one or two exceptions that was how it was.

Occasionally a girl wanted more and told me she had feelings for me, but I had to explain I was not emotionally available, which was the truth. There was no way I could have had a relationship at that point in time; I was mentally spent just trying to function.

I had a lot of sexual encounters I can't even remember, because I was so high on weed, and equally there were plenty of women I chatted to and never met up with. Sometimes I was too nervous to let them see me in the flesh. I felt self-conscious about putting on weight, and sometimes I insisted on keeping my tee shirt on during sex, because I felt so fat and disgusting.

A few women eventually went to the press with kiss-and-tell stories, which was very upsetting and embarrassing. One said I kept my white socks on, which has haunted me ever since. It might well have happened; I wouldn't put it past me. Maybe it was a northern thing; maybe I was cold? I can laugh about it now, but at the time I was mortified and felt terrible for my family, and especially my mum and sisters. It was a nightmare for them. They'd been so proud, and now they had to deal with my public humiliation. Neve was twelve and in secondary school, and I think she suffered more than anyone because kids were constantly asking her about me and taking the piss about stories they'd read. I started to ignore text messages and phone calls from the family because I couldn't face them, which compounded my loneliness and feelings of isolation.

I became as addicted to sex as I was to weed, and despite the bad press I didn't curb my recklessness. I couldn't. I craved sex, I had to have it and I needed it to fill the void and make myself feel better.

Another girl told a tabloid newspaper she slept with me at a party at my flat and claimed she was a prostitute. Someone else said I'd slept with her friend who was just seventeen, and there was even a story about me eating pizza during sex. I would never knowingly have slept with a prostitute or a seventeen-year-old, or eaten a Domino's during sex for that matter, but it could have happened. I was so off my head on weed and pills and sometimes alcohol too that any of these things could have happened when I was oblivious to the facts or to any kind of reality. I'm deeply ashamed to admit that, but it's the truth.

Scarily, there are whole parties that took place at my flat that I have no recollection of. I was in the dark on every level. I had no idea where I was or what I was doing on far too many occasions. It's so frightening to me now, not knowing what's true or how many women I slept with. Unfortunately, what I do remember is how little I cared about how much the women enjoyed themselves. I'd never been like that in bed before and even at the time, in the cold light of day, my behaviour shocked me. The morning after I'd feel even more disgusting, and then of course I needed more validation, and so I kept going, texting the next girl and the next.

For a long time, I tried to kid myself I was only doing what any young guy in my position would do, and I also wondered if my extremely high sex drive had something to do with any of the medication I was on. It didn't. The simple fact is I have an addictive personality coupled with a high sex drive, and that made me a sex addict.

At that time in my life I didn't mind the addiction, to be honest, because I was single. I didn't ever think about the future and how this would affect me if I fell in love and started a proper relationship. That was one problem I didn't have to face, not yet.

# CHAPTER FIFTEEN

*Dawson likes my voice. Wow.*
*Maybe I really do have talent*

I didn't confide in any of my friends about what life was like at home. By now I'd moved on from the skater crowd and got in with a group of lads who played football, drank cider on a Friday night and listened to indie music.

*I can't go to my mates. What would they think? It's too humiliating. They'll think I'm scruffy. I can't have that.*

I was already doing the indie thing before it became really popular, and that was how I was allowed into the group. I was starting to play the guitar too, which gave me kudos with the boys.

'Why don't you get a proper guitar and learn how to play?' one of Mam's boyfriends had said one day, when he saw me for the umpteenth time playing air guitar.

'I can't afford one,' I replied.

With that he went and bought me a second-hand acoustic guitar from the charity shop for about £30. I was obsessed by Nirvana and all the cool, grungy bands like Slipknot and Stereophonics. As soon as I picked up the guitar I wanted to compose songs and pretend I was Kurt Cobain. I already had the long hair too. I hid behind it and pulled my fringe over my dodgy right eye. I also loved Oasis and the Libertines, and I wanted to play and write music like they did.

'You need to learn to play first, before you start composing,' one of Mam's friends, Chris, said. 'I'll show you a couple of chords if you like.'

After a brief demonstration from Chris I worked out very quickly that for rock and grunge music you can make chords very easily by tuning the guitar to a drop D, putting one finger on a fret then moving it around the fret board.

I taught myself Nirvana's 'Smells Like Teen Spirit' and the next time Chris came around I showed him what I could do.

'He's already overtaken you by a country mile, Chris,' Mam laughed.

'Bloody hell! He's ten times better than me in a week and I've been playing for years! That boy has a musical ear.'

Instead of concentrating on learning the guitar properly I was already starting to write songs. The melodies were all heartbreaking or depressing, with me moaning about life. I listened to loads of Oasis and taught myself 'Wonderwall', which only uses four chords. That opened up the door to thousands of other songs, because I discovered those same few chords are the foundation of ninety per cent of pop music.

Now there was no stopping me. I'd be strumming whenever I could, putting those chords in different sequences and patterns and writing loads of songs.

When I went out with the indie lads on a Friday night I'd take my guitar and provide the entertainment. That was my role in the group, although I never felt I fully belonged. Just like with the skater kids, I felt I wasn't the most liked and was always the one who was a bit different to the rest. I was convinced I didn't connect with everyone in the way the rest of the lads connected with each other, and even with no evidence to support it I was constantly paranoid, thinking I was being slagged off behind my back, or that somebody had it in for me.

I was the awkward one, the socially inept one. I was on the outside looking in. As a result, I tried too hard to fit in and I saw friendships as a really big deal: they were like a blood tie, they were for life. That's how I felt, because I was so desperate for any validation I could get that I was not such a misfit after all. The trouble was, this group of lads thrived on banter, which basically revolved around picking on each other, and I was no good with that. I was too sensitive and insecure, and if anyone made a remark about me it would stab me in the heart and completely crush me.

Personal comments about my looks were the worst. They would take me straight back to being a little boy, being bullied at primary school for being bong-eyed. The turn in my eye was even more noticeable in secondary school, and it made all social situations hard for me. While I was talking to the lads, or to anyone, I'd often see a repulsive image of myself in my head, and instead of listening to what people were saying I'd have an internal dialogue running through my mind.

*They are seeing a really repulsive image. Is that why they just swapped glances? What are they looking at? What are they thinking? I feel like shit. I don't belong here.*

When Mam threw me out of the house there was no way I was going to ask any of my mates if I could stay at theirs; if I showed them this side of my life I'd feel like even more of an awkward outsider.

I walked the streets for a while on the night she chucked me out, wondering whether to try my dad but quickly dismissing the idea. I knew it wouldn't be convenient for him and I didn't want any more rejection. I'd asked before if I could stay with Dad, when I'd had bad rows with Mam, and he'd explained that, unfortunately, he had no room. They already had Jackie's niece staying with them, so there was nowhere for me to sleep.

'Sorry son, you know I'd put you up if I could.'

'Don't worry, Dad,' I always said, making out it was no big deal, even though it was. I wanted him to put me before Jackie's niece, or to at least say I could sleep on his sofa, but I couldn't say that to him. I always wanted my dad to think I was strong and capable. I didn't want his pity, I wanted his approval. I even used to pretend I liked Rangers much more than I did, because I wanted to please him as much as possible.

I eventually found a bench in a bit of secluded parkland not far from home, waited until it was dark and curled up for the night. It was freezing cold and I was scared to be out there alone, but I did get a bit of sleep. I felt so exhausted, so drained. I wanted to close my eyes and never have to open them. I didn't want to face what tomorrow would bring, because life was so bad. I had a sense of not belonging anywhere. I was an orphan; that's how I felt, sleeping on that bench.

When I eventually went home Sian let me in, warily. Mam was in bed, where she'd been all day.

'Can't you just stop arguing with Mam?' Sian snapped. 'What's the point, James? Just ignore it if she winds you up.'

'No I can't ignore this. What's going on is wrong. We should not be living in fear in our own house. We should not be unhappy. Mam needs help. She's clearly very troubled. It's not normal to be in bed all day or to go on benders like she does.'

I wanted to be a good person. I wanted to be the male role model, to fill the void left by Ronnie. To my mind, ignoring what was going on was not an option. I wanted to fix things, but getting involved just put me at the centre of the drama, over and over again.

When Mam eventually appeared, she went off at me, demon-style, shouting about all the things she hated about me. I'd let her down, just like my dad. I was aggressive and angry and argumentative. I was a nasty, bad person who brought nothing but trouble. I wasn't welcome in the house, she had no room for me, she didn't want to see my face.

I retaliated, screaming back at her, and she threw me out again. I could hardly blame her this time. I was very aggressive, punching walls, kicking furniture and calling her a bitch at the top of my voice. All my sisters were upset, which made me even more angry.

*Well done, Mam. You've done it again. You've wound me up by telling me I'm just like my dad and I've fallen for it, yet again. I'm your scapegoat, and now you can tell your girls and all your friends that it's all my fault. James is angry and aggressive and out of control. That's why we can't have him in the house.*

This time I eventually crept back to the house after walking around the neighbourhood for hours, but I didn't go inside. Instead I slept on the bench in Mam's back garden. Then I got the hell out of there as early as I could the next day, before she saw me, and I went to one of the local supermarkets to get some food. I had no money so I grabbed a carrier bag and threw a few sandwiches and snacks in when nobody was looking, then I just walked out, carrying my stolen breakfast.

The more I fell out with my mam the bigger the divide grew between me and Sian, and also between me and Jasmin.

It felt like Mam was pitting Jazz against me now, which hurt so deeply. In Bahrain Mam was always telling people how Jazz and I had an extra-strong bond, and it was true. I absolutely adored Jazz and felt very protective over her. When she was eight weeks old she got whooping cough, and ended up in special care. I can remember it incredibly clearly – it's one of those defining moments I can visualise in fine detail. On the same day that Jazz went into hospital I was having grommets put in my ears for the first time, and so I wasn't allowed to see her. I was absolutely heartbroken and cried my eyes out, and then it got worse. In the early hours of the morning Jazz's little heart stopped beating and the doctors had to put paddles on her to get her breathing again. I was distraught, and when she finally came home I wouldn't let Jazz out of my sight.

As she got older I was permanently in awe of Jazz because of her intelligence and feisty character. She is super-sharp, and she also has a bit of a maverick streak, which I could identify with. I remember one time she took herself off to swim in the sea and had to be rescued. A police officer brought her home and we were all flabbergasted, because she was only young. Jazz was a force to be reckoned with and you never quite knew what she would do next.

'Get out!' Jazz screamed at me. 'You can't stay here!'

She was spitting the words and flipping out, exactly like Mam.

'Jazz, I adore you. You're my little sister. Why are you saying this? I've done nothing wrong.'

'Just get out! We don't want you here!'

She was eight years old, and mimicking Mam.

It was heartbreaking and very difficult to comprehend. I get it now. The house was a battlefield and as a vulnerable little girl Jazz naturally needed to be on the side of the most power-ful person, and that was Mam. Meanwhile I was cast in the role of the big bad brother and the aggressive male.

I started to develop a theory about this, involving my mum's mum, who lived nearby. When I was little Nanna was very nurturing and maternal, just like my dad's mum in Scotland. She would roll through our door like a ball of positive energy, always carrying a bag of treats, and I'd be all over her and chatting non-stop, as I always did when any visitors came into the house. Nanna had a sweet and kind way of talking, and she would gently tell me to calm myself down while she got me a toffee or a gobstopper or a piece of her homemade Stottie bread. She was how I imagined every mam or nanna should be, and I loved being around her.

However, I learned more about Nanna as I grew up. She had six brothers, and when their mam died she had to look after them all. She was treated like a skivvy, and then when she married and had her own kids Nanna got a raw deal all over again, because my mam's dad was not around. Nanna developed a bitterness towards men and was on her own, through choice, for many years.

My theory was that Nanna's attitude had inflamed my mam's reaction to the breakdown of both her marriages. Just like Nanna, I reckoned Mam had an issue with men, and she was bitter towards them. She despised my dad and now she hated Ronnie, and she seemed completely unable to move on from everything that had happened to her. In fact, it was as if Mam grew more and more resentful as time went by, and she absolutely could not leave the past behind. The two divorces coloured her whole view of the world. The two men she once loved had both proven what Nanna had been saying for years. Men were unreliable. They would treat you badly and leave you in the lurch. You were better off without them, because men were bad news.

I was starting to see just how damaging this outlook, and Mam's inability to stop raking up the past, was to her mental health. She would descend into rants and laments that lasted for hours on end, dwelling on her terrible life and how badly she had been wronged by the men who were meant to stand by her. It was so unhealthy, and now it was damaging all of us kids in a major way.

I was the one who got it in the neck the most because Mam permanently saw my dad when she looked at me, but the truth was that we were all getting messed up by her – or should I say, by her mental illness. Neve wasn't getting the care and attention she needed as a toddler. Jazz was acting out as a mini version of Mam, which was disturbing, and

Sian was living in fear, scared of speaking out and being true to herself.

'Isn't that right, Sian?' Mam would ask, after telling her friends on the phone all about how much trouble I'd caused, usually in exaggerated, overly dramatic detail. 'Isn't that what James did?'

'Yes, Mam,' Sian would say flatly, because she knew that if she argued World War Three would break out.

Mam was seriously ill. None of this was her fault; I know this now. She was in the grip of her borderline personality disorder, but at that time I didn't understand mental health issues and I was so, so angry with her, rather than with her illness. I was too young to question what medical help she needed, or even to communicate with Sian about just how much of a crisis we were in. Instead I internalised all my hurt and anger.

Being thrown out of the house became a regular occurrence. I would walk the streets for hours, wallowing in my pain and allowing my resentment towards Mam to multiply so much it felt like my heart was crushing all my internal organs, pushing all life and hope out of me. Once she even threw me out on Christmas Day, telling me she didn't care where I went.

'What am I supposed to do, Mam?'

'Go to your mates, I don't care.'

'How can I do that on Christmas Day?'

I just walked around on my own, looking in windows and seeing other families all warm and happy inside their homes.

Music became my coping mechanism. I could vocalise my angst through my songs, and that's why I was writing all the time and singing and playing my guitar at every opportunity. It was my release and my therapy.

I was developing a bit of a reputation in the neighbourhood for my music, and one day a lad called Michael Dawson knocked on my door.

'I've heard you can sing. Come to my house and sing us a song then.'

My heart thumped. Dawson was a year older than me and was a known bully. When I was younger he'd come and kick the ball away when I was playing football with my mates, and he was always the kid who had money for the corner shop when nobody else did, and would walk past with Irn-Bru and big bags of sweets, teasing everyone but never sharing.

Randomly, he'd invited me to his house a few times in the past, once when he had a new arcade machine and wanted someone to play it with him. I went along because Dawson was so big and was such an alpha-male type that you didn't dare say no to him. There was no difference now; if I didn't sing for him I thought he might whack me.

'OK,' I said.

I can't remember what I sang but I'll never forget how nervous I felt, performing just for him. My heart was beating fast and I could feel my nerves snapping around my body.

'That's cool. You're very good.'

I exhaled with relief. Dawson's words gave me a massive boost. This was the biggest, toughest kid on the block speaking to me, and Dawson didn't dish out compliments lightly.

*Dawson likes my voice. Wow. Maybe I really do have talent.*

I smiled, which wasn't something I'd done for a while, and when I look back now I think how beautiful and unpredictable life can be. Dawson is now my best friend and of course the same guy whose sofa I slept on before judges' houses and the live shows.

There is always a chink of light and hope in the darkness, though I didn't see life that way back then. I was buried too deep.

# CHAPTER SIXTEEN

*If you lose it all you won't have to deal with all this stress. If you lose it all life will be easier*

'Can you please remove that dancer from the set? She's too distracting.'

I was making the video for my new single, 'You're Nobody 'Til Somebody Loves You', and this was a flirty chat-up line, because the dancer I was pointing at was absolutely stunning – so perfect she looked Photoshopped in broad daylight.

The blonde-haired girl was mortified for a moment because she thought I was genuinely firing her, but when she realised it was a joke she stuck her tongue out at me cheekily. We were doing a twelve-hour shoot on a street in east London and when we took a break for lunch I tried to make conversation, telling the dancer I liked her pink velour trousers.

'I didn't choose them,' she said, smiling.

The girl's name was Jessica Grist, and after the shoot I went up and asked her friend if I could have her number.

Jess came over to me and was quite flirty in return. 'Do you talk to all the girls like this? Is that what you do – you get a girl's friend to get her number?'

I told her this wasn't my style normally, which was true. There was something about Jess I really liked. She seemed different to other girls, I really did want her number and thought that was the best way of going about it. Thankfully she gave it to me, and I texted her that night. I was excited when Jess texted back straight away, but I could tell she was wary of me. She wouldn't meet me and said she just wanted to be friends.

'I don't get involved with anyone in the business,' she said. Jess had worked extremely hard to become a professional dancer. She'd gone to the Royal Ballet School and was at the top of her game, and this was her rule.

'I won't give up,' I told her. 'I like you, a lot.'

I know now that the real reason Jess wouldn't meet me was because of all the stories that had appeared in the press about me and other girls. Hardly surprisingly, she thought I was a player, but she was also confused, because she says I didn't seem to be the same person she'd read about in the papers.

We were both really busy, but over the next few months I kept texting Jess, telling her I still wanted to see her. She was dancing all over the country and I was working hard on my album, which I was finding very stressful. I had to strike a balance between making something the *X Factor* fans would like and being true to myself in my music. My A&R at Syco – the person responsible for overseeing my artistic development – didn't seem to like my rap stuff or anything that was left of field or a bit too raw and honest. I felt disconnected from him and he just didn't seem to get me. I was very frustrated because I kept thinking about what Gary Barlow had told me, about not letting anyone change me. I developed a bit of a rebellious, Eminem streak and began writing songs about how my A&R was controlling my music. It seems quite funny now, but back then it was deadly serious; I felt patronised, compromised and trapped, but I was also in a dark headspace so couldn't comprehend anything he was suggesting. The other challenge was that I was also going through a steep learning curve about the music business generally, discovering how everything in the industry has to work for the label's marketing plans, and finding out I had no control over decisions made at the top of the chain.

It didn't help that at the same time as making the album I was getting my teeth straightened, which I'd promised myself I'd do as soon as I had some money. It was a long-winded process and the train tracks in my mouth affected the way I sang, making me feel I couldn't give my all vocally.

It wasn't all bad, of course. Thanks to my record deal I had hundreds of thousands of pounds in my bank account, and one of the first things I did was take eight of my mates on holiday to Miami, which was wild.

'Pick what you like,' I said to Dawson and all the lads when we went into the Apple store. They were coming out with Apple Macs and Beats and I loved seeing their faces. We drank champagne in all the best clubs and casinos and I'd drop £5,000 on the roulette table, lose the lot and walk away with a shrug. I have absolutely no regrets about the trip, because we'll still be talking about it when we're old men.

Money had never meant anything to me. When I was a teenager, if I got £100 for a gig in a pub I'd buy all the lads beer and pizza, even though the following week I'd have nothing left and would end up shoplifting food from Tesco to survive. It was the same now. I had absolutely no money management skills. I thought I was set up for life and that the cash from my record deal would never run out.

*If you lose it all you won't have to deal with all this stress. If you lose it all life will be easier. Throw it all away. See if you can. Then you can do it again, and do it your way.*

This was the voice of a very deep-rooted demon in my head. He had been there, in my subconscious, ever since I won *The X Factor*. He knew I had a bit of a chip on my shoulder because I got my record deal through a TV talent show, and he knew I was struggling with my A&R and was afraid of compromising my integrity. He also knew how freaked out I was by the overnight success and the strange new life I was living.

*What's real? Who's real? Who cares about you? What if you lost it all? Who would still be there? There is only one way to find out, James. Lose everything, I dare you.*

I moved out of Kensal Rise and got myself a penthouse flat in Hammersmith. It was very cool but a bit pretentious; the type of place I thought I ought to live in, rather than one I was really at home in. I felt a bit trapped there, being high up, which didn't help when I suffered an anxiety attack and needed to get outside and breathe.

Jazz was sharing a bedroom with Neve at Mam's house and things were not great at home. Mam was up and down again and I wanted to protect Jazz as much as I could. I knew exactly what it was like being a teenager around Mam when she wasn't in a good place, and so I invited Jazz to come and stay with me. She moved into the flat with her boyfriend at the time, and it felt like a win–win, because not only did it help her out, but I got a bit of home and a reminder of reality. I loved having my little sister around.

There was another benefit too: Jazz's boyfriend liked a smoke, and we'd all just hang out, smoking weed and playing video games like Olympics or WWE wrestling. Me and Jazz would reminisce about being kids, when I used to pretend I was Stone Cold Steve Austin and slam her on the bed doing 'rock bottoms'. It was grounding to have her around and we had loads of fun nights, playing so many video games Jazz had blisters on her hands from pressing the controls.

'Just give me a minute.'

Every night I'd hit a point where I got palpitations, felt super-anxious and had to duck outside because I could feel a panic attack coming on. I'd take myself for a walk and tell myself to breathe. I tried to shield Jazz as much as I could from my depression and all of my mess, but she knew what was going on and always did her best to support me. I felt pressure from that, because I desperately wanted to be the protective big brother, but the reality was I was not the best role model and that made me feel guilty.

I was smoking so much weed I'd be zombified at the end of the night, and then I'd take a dozen joints to bed with me and smoke them one after the other until I knocked myself out completely. I was also still taking antidepressants and sleeping tablets. I'd stayed on the three lots of pills I'd been prescribed during *The X Factor*, and I couldn't do without them. I didn't even dare try.

When I finished working on my album I enjoyed having more time to do my own thing musically, and I really got into my rap. I'd only managed to get sixteen bars onto the album and was disappointed by that. I was a big fan of Charlie Sloth's rap shows on Radio 1 and Radio 1Xtra and it was my ambition to do *Fire In The Booth*, as it's a rap purist show and carries a lot of prestige. No *X Factor* winner had ever been in the booth. I wanted to be the first, and to show people what I could do.

Jess finally agreed to see me around this time. I'd refused to give up. We'd been texting for three or four months and there was a good connection there. She started coming over to the flat and right from the start I felt comfortable and happy to be with her and just knew we'd be together. It was surprising, really, as on the face of it we had nothing in common and came from totally different worlds. Jess grew up in a very middle-class family. She spoke really well, was super-fit and clean-living and didn't smoke weed; in fact she disapproved of it and was quite passive-aggressive with me about my habit.

Despite our differences, we somehow got each other and hit it off. I think one of the things that bonded us was that Jess told me her dad had suffered from mental illness and died when she was in her teens, which was an extremely shocking event in her life. She'd suffered panic attacks in the past and understood them. I found myself opening up to Jess, and falling in love with her.

By now I'd finally come to terms with what happened with Rita Ora. I'd gone from feeling heartbroken when she suddenly went cold on me to being quite bitter and resentful towards her; I felt as though she'd played with me. I wrote a rap about her, to help me deal with my feelings, and I decided to perform it on *Fire In The Booth*, when I got my chance to go on the show. It seemed like a good idea at the time although one of the lines was, 'Some people's Oras and demeanours can deceive us, but what they really want is a piece of your penis.' I think I needed to get that off my chest. I was stoned when I performed it and wasn't worried at all because I knew the lyrics were extremely mild compared to what can be said in the booth. My only intention was to make an impression with my rapping, but the fact I was rapping about Rita was picked up by the press and created a bit of a storm. Rita herself got in touch and was pretty upset, although I managed to smooth that over, as she's cool like that.

It was a different story with the media. I was slated, and I was so confused by that.

*What the hell? This is rap. Anything goes in the booth. Why don't people understand that?*

I was genuinely puzzled, which shows how I'd lost my grip on reality. I had no idea how much damage I was doing to my reputation and my career. I was starting on my path of self-destruction, but I couldn't see it, not at all.

My behaviour wasn't going down well with Syco. I'd already been called in for a meeting because this wasn't my only misdemeanour. I'd got into trouble for tweeting something about One Direction being more about marketing than music. Syco told me to clean up my act, but unfortunately, I didn't listen.

A rapper called Micky Worthless mocked me on Twitter for going in the booth, and then put out a 'diss' track called 'Stay in Your Lane', slagging me off for coming from *The X Factor*, saying I didn't deserve to go in the booth and calling me a faggot. I retaliated by recording my own hip-hop diss track on my phone, just rapping off the top of my head. I put it online a few hours later, cheered on by a few of my mates. We were all stoned apart from Jess, who told me not to do it, but I didn't listen. Our relationship was very new and she didn't have the power to stop me, even though she could see how dangerous this was.

'Don't worry about it,' I told Jess. 'Honestly, anything goes in the context of rap. It's just a rap battle. Far worse rap battles take place all the time.'

My scheme was, 'Hey Micky, why you always talking about me, do you fancy me?' and in one of the lines I asked if he was 'queer' – a big mistake, and something I'm very embarrassed about. It quickly got picked up online, but instead of recognising when to stop and apologise to anyone I'd offended, I threw myself into a full-on Twitter spat with Worthless.

I was unrepentant, even when other people joined in. Despite the growing backlash, I remained convinced that as everything I'd said was in the context of a rap battle, I had done absolutely nothing wrong and had nothing to say sorry for. What I completely failed to realise was that the rules were very different for me compared to other rappers. I was the winner of *The X Factor*, and I was being judged as such. It was no defence at all to say I was rapping and therefore could say whatever I wanted, or that I should be judged like all other rappers. I had a massive fan base. My new album had just gone to number two in the charts – it went on to sell 400,000 copies. And, most importantly, Syco had already warned me to stay out of trouble.

Even when I got a concerned phone call from the US, I failed to realise how misjudged and dangerous my behaviour was. Russell Eslamifar had looked after publicity on *The X Factor* and now worked on American *X Factor*. We hadn't kept in touch after the show but I knew Russell had always rated me very highly and had my best interests at heart.

'James, what are you doing?' he said.

'What do you mean, man?'

'Get yourself off Twitter. You're going to ruin your career.'

'OK mate, listen I've just had a joint . . .'

I was so high it didn't register with me that I should listen to Russell. As well as smoking weed I was popping Valium and drinking a lot every day, so my head was completely fogged. Russell knew the business inside out. He knew me, and he'd taken the trouble to call from the US when he really didn't have to, as he was no longer officially involved in my career in any way. I should have had huge alarm bells going off in my head but I was so stoned and deluded I just put the phone down and didn't give Russell's words or warning a second thought. Instead, all day long I carried on blindly justifying why I had responded to Worthless's diss track in the way I had.

When I woke up the next day and looked at my Twitter feed, all hell had broken loose. I was public enemy number one. My old nemesis Frankie Boyle waded in to slag me off, and all the papers were carrying stories about my 'homophobic rant'.

'This is insane!' I cried to Jess. I was stunned, and petrified about what would happen next. 'Are these people for real? This is a diss rap and I'm not homophobic. I lived with Rylan, for god's sake. Nobody could be more gay than him and I love him to bits! How the hell could anyone accuse me of being homophobic? It simply isn't true.'

However much I protested, I was starting to see I was not going to win this one. Using the word 'queer', in any context, was career suicide for me. The fact I am not homophobic was irrelevant. I'd said that word, I'd offended people and I couldn't take it back. I knew I was done for. I'd made a huge mistake and it was out there, for the whole country to hear and read about. My manager, Caroline, had been away for the weekend and missed the whole thing. When she caught up with what had happened she helped arrange for me to put out an apology, but it was too little, too late. Embarrassingly, Syco then took control of my Twitter account. I'd been such a fool and it was all my own fault. It was absolutely devastating.

*Avoid the spaces in between.*

I could feel myself slipping through the biggest crack ever. My album began falling down the charts and, after requests from customers, iTunes began giving out refunds to anyone offended by me. *Offended by me.* It was so mortifying. I'd spent my whole life worrying what people thought of me, wondering if they thought I was a weirdo or a misfit and wanting to fit in.

*Look at what you've done. You're repulsive. You offend people. You're out of control, James. We don't want you here. You're nothing but trouble.*

I felt like my whole life was in free fall. Then Lucy Spraggan – one of my fellow *X Factor* contestants – had a go at me. I texted her to find out why, asking if it was because she's a gay activist and she felt she had to. Our text conversation descended into a row and she later posted the texts on Twitter, which hammered another nail into my coffin. I should have known better than to get involved, but I didn't.

*Your career is dead and you are going to die, James. Face it, you're a loser and you always have been. Look over there! Can you see it? That's your body, dead on the floor. You're finished. Your life is over.*

I started having panic attacks several times a day. I'd be gasping for air while the voices screamed louder and louder in my head. As soon as I got my breath back I'd reach for another joint. As always, this was my escape route from trouble and the real world. I carried on smoking myself into oblivion, every single time.

That was what my life was now. Oblivion. A very large space in between. It was terrifying, because I had no idea if I'd survive.

# CHAPTER SEVENTEEN

*This was meant to be a
crossroads, not a dead end*

'Would you be prepared to have your son for four days a week and would you, Mr Arthur, be happy to have James for three days?'

I was sitting at a table in a Social Services office in town with Mam, Dad and a social worker, and this was a major crossroads in my life. I'd been given a social worker because I was very obviously falling through the cracks at school, and things had got so bad at home I'd asked Social Services to fix up this review meeting, with both my parents present. I was still only fourteen years old and at this moment I really needed my parents to step up to the plate and be there for me. I hoped this crisis meeting would make them realise how unhappy I was, and that we could all get to a better place.

Mam and Dad were on opposite sides of the table, with me in the middle of them. I hadn't seen them in the same room as each other for years and, as always, they weren't speaking to one another. It was such an uncomfortable, daunting situation but I had to bring things to a head like this, as I couldn't carry on living with Mam full-time any longer. I was at breaking point. The rows were too wild, her moods too erratic. She was throwing me out too often, I was sick of sleeping on benches and my education was suffering, just at a time when I really needed to knuckle down.

After I'd been repeatedly thrown out by my mum, Dad had eventually bought a bed for me, which he crammed in his back dining room. There was nowhere else to put me as they still had Jackie's niece living with them. Sleeping in the dining room was better than being on a bench, but it was only ever an ad hoc arrangement, and because of that I never felt very comfortable. Also, Jackie was very house-proud and liked set routines. I wasn't used to living in a house where you felt frowned on if you didn't wash up immediately after tea, wipe splashes off the washbasin after you used it or go to bed at a set time every night. I can see now that Jackie just had decent standards and liked a certain level of discipline, and there's nothing wrong with that. But all of this was so alien to me, and I felt like I wasn't good enough when I didn't live the way everyone else did in the bungalow. At best I felt like a visitor, at worst a burden, and I needed that to change. I resented

Jackie a lot because, rightly or wrongly, I blamed her for this whole set-up, and for being a barrier between me and my dad.

I hoped that if the arrangement was formalised by Social Services I might feel more at home at Dad and Jackie's. It was a drastic step for me to bring the meeting about, but something had to give, because I desperately needed my life to improve.

I held my breath when the social worker explained all of this and then asked my parents if they would be prepared to commit to having me for part of the week each.

'Yes, that's fine,' Dad said immediately.

'No,' Mam said. 'I don't want him any time.'

I didn't react; I just felt numb.

*My mam doesn't want me, any time. She was meant to step up to the plate and help me be happier. This wasn't meant to happen. This was meant to be a crossroads, not a dead end.*

I looked at Mam and listened as she explained why she didn't want me, and her words killed me.

Mam claimed she couldn't cope with my anger and aggression. She said she had no room for me anyway and repeated she didn't want me any time, not even half the week. I was upsetting my sisters and disrupting all their lives. She didn't want anything to do with me.

I couldn't understand why Mam was saying this. I did have some terrible rows with her and I wasn't exactly a model pupil at school, but I wasn't that bad. I wasn't beating people up. I wasn't doing drugs or getting into trouble with the police. Why couldn't she cope with me?

Also, the reason I argued with Mam was because *she* was constantly going on at me about my dad, dragging me down and making me feel like a bad person. I had to stick up for myself and I couldn't let her get away with her behaviour in the house, because it wasn't normal or healthy. I wanted my sisters to have a better life. Ultimately, I wanted us all to have some kind of happiness, but look where it had got me. It was a massive kick in the teeth to have her blame *me* for the situation at home.

*Why is this happening? What have I done that is so wrong? Why am I such a misfit? Why don't I belong anywhere?*

The chatter in my head was drowning out some of the things my parents and the Social Services people were saying, but what I did hear, loud and clear, was that I would have to go into part-time foster care. My social worker was adamant I couldn't stay with Dad and Jackie full-time as they had no proper bedroom for me, so this was my only option.

'James can stay with you for three days a week, Mr Arthur, and we will arrange respite care for the other half of the week.'

*Respite care? Fuck all of you!*

I wanted my dad to stand up and fight for me. I wanted him to say, 'No way. You're my son, and you're coming to live with me, full-time. I don't care what Social Services say. I'll sort it out.'

He didn't. He listened to what the social workers said about me sleeping in his dining room and how that was not acceptable as a full-time arrangement. He and Mam had never agreed on anything before, but now they were in unison. They both signed the papers that put me into voluntary foster care.

*You two are my parents and you can't wait to get rid of me. I'm going into foster care. Fuck you! This was not meant to happen, no way. Why did I even bring this meeting about?*

I was so shocked and scared at the thought of going into care, and then everything happened so fast. Dad drove me to my new foster home in Brotton, about ten miles from Redcar. This is one of those traumatic moments I've blanked out of my mind. I have no recollection of packing my bags, travelling to Brotton or even of saying goodbye to Dad when he dropped me off. Instead there are black spots, massive black spots.

I realise now I was shutting down emotionally. At this pivotal moment in my life, when I needed my parents more than I'd ever needed them before, neither of them was there for me. I couldn't take any of this in because it was just too painful. The way I saw it, Dad had put Jackie's niece before me, and that did so much damage. As for Mam, she was a person I didn't even recognise any more, which in hindsight is hardly surprising: she was going through a period of severe clinical depression, and had a major nervous breakdown after her second divorce. She was subsequently hospitalised for six weeks.

I do recall sitting in my new bedroom, looking at a picture of my sisters I'd brought with me and crying my eyes out. Mam and Dad – the two most important people in my life – had let me down catastrophically. I was an orphan, an abandoned child, a misfit, a bad person, a failure, a loser. My life was shattered and the pieces could never be put back, not properly.

I switched something off in my head and shut myself away so I didn't have to face any more trauma or listen to any more chatter in my brain about what a worthless piece of shit I was and how my life was so miserable and pointless.

The foster home was out in the countryside. The locals wore rigger boots and tracksuits and said things like, 'I'm going t' pub' or 'I'm off buying cockles from shop.' To a townie like me, they were country bumpkins. I was dressed like Eminem, because I was into his music in a big way. I must have stuck out like a sore thumb but I didn't care. Even though I was terrified of being in a place I didn't know, with strangers, at least I was not dealing with rejection here. I was welcomed by my foster carers. I wasn't living in fear of Mam's black moods, and I wasn't feeling like I was in the way in Dad's bungalow.

*I feel more at home in this house of strangers than I do at my mam's or my dad's. How has this happened? It must be my fault. This isn't normal. This is odd.*

My foster carers had two sons around my age and a couple of other lads staying with them long term. They also provided emergency respite care, so there would be lots of different kids coming and going. The juveniles on emergency placements came from proper broken homes and tragic backgrounds, and by that, I mean they'd maybe suffered abuse or had severe behavioural or emotional problems their parents couldn't deal with. In some cases, their parents were dead or in prison, and there was nobody in their world capable of looking after them. I felt totally disconnected from those kids; they came from a world I didn't recognise.

*At least they have a better reason than me to be here. At least their parents have a good reason for letting this happen.*

In the beginning, I stayed at the foster home for four nights a week and at my dad's for three, but I was still never happy sleeping in Dad and Jackie's dining room. In fact, I felt like even more of an intruder than I had before, because now this was a regular arrangement it seemed like I was putting Jackie out more than ever. I'm sure she didn't mean to make me feel that way, but I never felt completely comfortable or welcome.

It was also really difficult to live out of two homes. I felt untethered, and on a practical level it wasn't helping me cope with school, because I was forever juggling clothes and books and sports kits between the two houses.

'I want to stay at the foster carers' full-time,' I told Dad. 'I think it's for the best.'

I'd only been in respite care for a couple of weeks, but I'd made my mind up.

'There's no need, son,' he said. 'We're happy to have you here, for the three days.'

I knew Dad meant it, and that he would have had me living with him all the time if his circumstances were different, but they weren't. As it was, it was three days or nothing, and it wasn't working for me. I tried to make it easy for Dad, insisting that I was doing what *I* wanted. It wasn't true, of course. What I really wanted was for him to insist I stay with him full-time, no matter what anybody else said, including the social workers. I never said that though, because there was no point.

'Honestly, Dad. I need one base. It's what I want, it's what's best for me.'

I was starting the last two years of school – the most important years – and I used this as part of my argument for needing the stability of having one place to call home, because I didn't want Dad to feel bad or guilty. I got my way, and that was it: I volunteered myself into full-time foster care. I was a full-time foster kid; that was my life now. When I moved all of my stuff in, I looked at my foster mum in a different way than before.

*She is my mum now. This is how it is now. She might be in my life forever. My mum won't be in it again, not ever.*

I began to truly believe that. I had no real mum any more,

just this fake mum. Mam had disowned me and I resigned myself surprisingly quickly to the fact I'd probably never see her again.

When I lay in my bedroom, looking at the furniture and curtains and duvet cover that didn't belong to me, I felt disturbed. Nothing held any history for me, and the smell and atmosphere of the room, and of the whole house, was so unfamiliar it alarmed me. I remembered landing in Dubai and being hit by a level of heat and humidity I'd never experienced before. That was unsettling, but in an exciting way. I was in a whole new world but I could cope with it, because I had my family around me. Come what may, I'd always have my family around me, to watch my back and keep me safe. That's what I thought.

Now I was just forty minutes away from Redcar on a bus, not a long-haul flight away, but the culture shock was so much bigger and I felt so incredibly lonely. I wanted my sisters. I wanted to wrestle with Jazz and make her laugh, I wanted to listen to Neve giggle and chatter and I wanted to hear Sian's music. Even to hear Sian telling me to shut up and stop arguing would have been better than this. I could hear the muffled sound of kids I didn't know in other rooms and unfamiliar noises from the fields outside. It was an alien soundtrack and it made me pine for familiarity and the comforts of being at home, surrounded by my family.

I turned my head and cried into my pillow, thinking about the past.

When I was eight and nine years old there were so many nights when I used to lie on my bunk bed in the back bedroom at Winchester Road, listening for hours to the *Legends of Football* Radio 5 Live phone-in and the *Love Line* phone-in on the local Century Radio, when guys would call in and talk about their problems.

Mam had a theory about that. She thought it comforted me to hear men talking together, because I was the only boy in the house. She could be right, and I definitely did enjoy being there in my bed, with the radio chattering in my ear. Even when Mam had upset me and I cried in my pillow, I felt so much better than I did now. At least then I had another chance the next day. It might be a good day, a day when I didn't step on the cracks in between the paving stones. Now I might as well walk on nothing but the cracks, because I had nothing to lose. Whatever happened, it was going to be a bad day, because my own family didn't want me, and how could it get any worse than that?

'Why are you getting on the bus that way, Raff?'

'Oh, I'm staying at my auntie's.'

It was a lie I repeated time and time again when I crossed the road after school and took the bus to Brotton, which was in the opposite direction to both my mam and dad's houses. I didn't want my friends to know I was in foster care. I was embarrassed by it because to my mind it made me a bit of a scruff bag. I also didn't want anyone to think my parents were bad people. It meant I was always hyper-alert to any remarks about stuff that went on outside of school, because I was so scared of the other kids finding out my secret.

The good thing was I was sticking in at school now. Somehow, I was getting a good night's sleep and I'd always get to school on time and do my best in class. In the evenings, I played pool and wrestled on the lawn with the other lads, plus I was in a five-a-side football team and played three times a week. I loved it, even though I'd usually have to wait an hour in the freezing cold to get the bus back to Brotton afterwards, as the service was so infrequent.

*I've got to go back to my fake family. All my mates are going back to their homes. Fuck.*

That's what I'd think when I sat at the bus stop on my own, but I was resigned to my fate. Mam didn't want me and Dad couldn't have me. I just had to get on with it now and accept my new life. I wrote a song with lyrics about going back to my fake family; it was a way of expressing myself, as I had nobody to talk to.

At weekends, I chose to hang out with my friends rather than visit my dad or my sisters. I was still in with the indie lads and one of them lived on a farm, so we'd go there and camp in the fields, putting up tents and lights to create a festival scene. I'd play the guitar and sing and we'd sit around drinking cans of Stella and trying to get wrecked. I had my first joint and smoked a few roll-up cigarettes – rollies as we called them – on Friday nights like that.

It was depressingly easy to cut myself off from my family. I'd see Sian around school sometimes but I wouldn't really speak to her. She'd become a huge goth and was quite a misfit at school, so I swerved her just like a lot of other kids did. I didn't feel guilty; I resented Sian for not backing me at home and I thought she didn't care about me.

Dad visited me in foster care once or twice, but I think it was only when there was a purpose rather than to spend any proper time together. Even at Christmas I stayed with my foster family, and I have no recollection of seeing my dad on my birthday or on any other special occasions. I definitely didn't see Mam and she never phoned me, not once. I was erased from her life, and I didn't visit my nanna either, because

Mam had told so many tales about my supposed violence and aggression that Nanna didn't want anything to do with me.

One night I went out camping with my pals, drank eight cans of Stella and finally told them my big secret.

'I'm a foster kid!' I blubbed. 'I'm a worthless piece of shit!'

I'd been in foster care for well over a year and was nearly sixteen years old at this point. I cried like a baby; it was such a relief to get this off my chest. My friends were so cool about it and told me I was not worthless at all. I still played the class clown at school and they told me I was great at making people laugh, and they all told me how good I was at singing and playing the guitar.

'You're amazing, Raff. You've got talent. You're just so good.'

I knew they meant what they said and their words comforted me. I had something to offer after all, but I still didn't feel great about myself. My reaction was just like the one I had after my triumph on stage as the modern Major-General in Bahrain, when Mam praised me to the hilt. Hearing my mates saying such encouraging things about me meant a lot and gave me a boost, but I still knew my place in the world. I was still a misfit and an oddball.

Deep down I knew that all I really had going for me was my music. Writing songs helped me deal with the past, and it was all I wanted to do in my future. Nothing else brought me anywhere close to happiness.

# CHAPTER EIGHTEEN

## *I want to be happy. I want to be healthy*

'I've made some very silly mistakes,' I told Dermot O'Leary, and several million TV viewers. 'And I just want to say sorry for abusing my position as an X *Factor* winner because I owe everything to this thing.'

I'd been invited back on the show in November 2013 to perform 'Recovery', the second single off my album, just weeks after my Twitter disgrace and online meltdown. The public had petitioned to get me off the show, and part of me wished they'd won, because that would get me out of this scary situation.

When I walked out on stage I felt like I did as a little boy, after I'd left Bahrain and had to walk into Rye Hills School, wondering if I was going to have my head flushed down the toilet.

*What a loser. You had it all and look what's happened. You're a joke. You're an oddball. What a total idiot. You misfit! You didn't deserve what you had. You don't deserve anything. You're worthless.*

I thought my performance was terrible and it didn't feel like any kind of turning point at all. I was a long way away from my personal recovery, and public opinion was fiercely divided over whether I should be given a second chance after my mistakes. I had a huge mountain to climb, just when I was feeling at my lowest ebb.

I don't know how I'd have survived if it weren't for Jess, and Jazz. If I had subconsciously pressed the self-destruct button in order to find out who was still there for me when everything turned to shit, I had my answer. It was Jess and Jazz, and a few of my best mates from home. The lads were always there, although because they were six hours away they didn't know the half of what I was going through.

'Jess, Jess, come and help me! I'm having a heart attack. Get me an ambulance, quick!'

'James, it isn't a heart attack, it's a panic attack. You need to breathe. Take deep breaths, try to focus on your breathing . . .'

'No Jess, you're wrong. It's a heart attack. It's gonna kill me. Feel my heart. It's going to burst out of my chest. Honestly, babe, I need an ambulance. Please call me an ambulance.'

'No, James. Remember this happened last night? You thought it was a heart attack, just like now, but it wasn't.

What you're experiencing is a panic attack and you just need to breathe and you will be able to control it. Shall we go for a walk? Come on, let's go outside. Let's get some air . . .'

*You're going to die, James. You can't survive this.*

'No! I can't. I can't breathe. Please Jess, don't let me die.'

Sometimes I'd try to argue with the demons in my head.

*Jess is right. I'm not dying. This isn't going to kill me really, is it? Surely it can't. I'm not dead yet. I'd be dead already if panic attacks could kill me. But even so . . .*

My argument was always too weak to ward off the screaming voices and Jess would be left with no choice but to call me an ambulance, because I'd be a gasping, pleading, paranoid wreck.

The sound of the approaching ambulance siren soothed me instantly. I was going to be saved and, as always, it was only when the paramedics checked me over and told me my heart was fine that I began to breathe normally again. The paramedics had become my safety blanket to such an extent that even if I heard an ambulance siren randomly in the street, racing to help someone else, in my messed-up head I'd feel safer.

Unfortunately, the more panic attacks I had, the more I lost sight of all positivity. Sometimes I'd be sitting there with Jess and it would just hit me: I didn't know where I was in life, and there was no point to my life. I'd lose it, spiral out of all control and have to call an ambulance. When Jess tried to reason with me there were times when my paranoia was so wild I questioned her motives and whether she was even real.

*What is a girl like her doing with someone like me? What is she gaining? She doesn't feel real. Nothing is real. My life is pointless and worthless.*

Some of the moments when Jess was there, trying to help me, were the loneliest, scariest moments I've ever been through. I should have been listening to her because she never failed to provide the loyal voice of reason, but instead I was convinced there was no one for me in this world.

I was so worried about my mistakes and my career and what was going to happen to me that when I came down from a panic attack I'd smoke more weed and take more pills to try to escape all my worries. It was the only way I could stop myself dwelling on the past and fearing the future.

My thought patterns were so negative that I'd look at Jess and think she made matters worse for me. I had a responsibility to her, and that was a pressure. I felt the same way towards my family, and especially Jazz.

*You can't mess things up. You have to get through this. You have to make a success of your career, and you have to be there for Jess and Jazz and everyone who loves you. It's all on your shoulders. Don't let them down.*

Most days I was taking 50mg of Sertraline in the morning and four Xanax plus a dose of Diazepam in the evening. By now I had a jar in the flat that was full of joints ready to smoke, and I rarely had a joint out of my hand. I'd smoke four or five immediately before bed then routinely take my dozen or so joints to bed with me and smoke them one after the other until I passed out. Sometimes I'd fall asleep with a joint in my mouth, which terrifies me now. My excuse was always that weed helped me with my anxiety, but really it made it worse. I was trapped in a vicious circle and was like a zombie all of the time.

I did my first tour from January to April 2014, which took me all round the UK and Europe. It should have been the pinnacle of my career so far, because performing live was what I loved more than anything. Of course, it wasn't. Jess came on tour with me and I've had to ask her what it was like, because I was so stoned I can barely remember any of it. She said I'd sleep all day, have a quick shower half an hour before I was due on stage, do the show and stay up all night, smoking weed and writing songs until I passed out. Jess remembers a few occasions when I misplaced my bag of 'meds' as we called them. I went into a meltdown, worrying about what would happen if I didn't take my antidepressants and panicking so much I couldn't catch my breath. Then I'd be sucked into a full-scale anxiety attack and would walk the streets for hours, or sprint at full pelt, to pull myself back down. I was wary of calling ambulances when I was abroad, and so my attacks lasted longer as I had to try to get through them by myself.

I was writing music all the time, often in the middle of the night when I couldn't sleep, and I made a mixtape called *All The World's A Stage*, which I released online during the tour. I later had that phrase tattooed across my chest, and I also had an upside-down cross done on my cheek, under my right eye. People asked me what the significance of the cross was, but the truth was I was so destroyed on weed and pills I couldn't even remember having it done; I was just rebelling, kicking out and doing what the hell I felt like.

One of the tracks on the mixtape – 'Follow the Leader' – was written from the point of view of a deranged fan who turned against me once they read I was allegedly homophobic. It was in the style of Eminem's hit 'Stan' and contained the line 'I'm gonna blow up your family like I'm a terrorist.' When I put it online I didn't think for one minute I was going to finally blow up my own career.

My phone rang when I was doing a radio interview in

Germany, at the end of the tour. It was Caroline, my manager, sounding deadpan.

'Syco has dropped you,' she said bluntly.

'What?' I stuttered. 'What do you mean?'

She explained that they were not happy about the terrorist line in 'Follow the Leader'. It seemed it was the final straw. Syco didn't want to stand by me any longer. I was viewed as a loose cannon.

'So . . . is that my career over?'

There was a pause.

'There's no way of telling.'

I was speechless, my heart shrivelled in fear and I had visions of seeing myself dead on the floor again. I was finished. I couldn't get up from this. Everything I'd ever worked for had been destroyed – and it was all my own stupid fault.

Jess consoled me and was incredibly supportive, which meant so much.

'What are you even doing with a loser like me?' I asked. 'Seriously, why?'

She told me how she felt about me. She said she loved me, but I didn't believe her. I thought I was going properly mad. I began questioning everything and it felt like bits of my mind were falling away, because I couldn't think logically. Every thought I had was laden with doom and fear. The foundations of my life had been smashed beneath my feet.

I thought back to when Ronnie left, and I recalled Mam's shocking words. 'He doesn't want anything to do with any of you. It's over. Forget about Ronnie. You'll never see him again.'

The same thing was happening now, except it wasn't Ronnie being ripped away from me so brutally. It was my recording contract, my career, my future. Everything I'd worked for.

I felt incredibly lonely and confused. In lucid moments I felt so grateful to have Jess supporting me, because I had put her through so much and she deserved better. The first time I'd told Jess I loved her was the night I was asked back on *The X Factor*, to make my apology and perform 'Recovery'. She was one of the dancers on the show that week, and she looked incredible.

'I'm officially in love,' I texted her, and it was true. I'd fallen in love with her, and I couldn't believe she was mine.

Unfortunately, despite the way we felt about each other, I couldn't help self-destructing in this area of my life too. I was so paranoid and messed up that even after I'd got with Jess I was still looking for validation from other women. I was addicted to texting girls and sharing sexually flirtatious messages with women online. I couldn't stop myself even though I knew it was crazy. I had massive trust issues because of what had happened in my childhood, and with my sudden fame, yet here I was, putting myself at so much risk, and all while I had a beautiful girlfriend.

Jess found out I was messaging girls. We talked for hours about how insecure I was about myself, and what made me behave that way. Jess was amazingly understanding, and most of the time I was completely baffled about why she bothered.

'Seriously, I'm not worth it. I'm a mess. You're a gorgeous girl. Look at you! You could do so much better than me. I don't want to hurt you.'

Unbelievably, even though I was the one playing with fire and Jess was being unstintingly loyal, I began to worry about whether I could trust *her*. Jess worked with male dancers all the time who had the most amazing physiques, while I was still overweight. I was eating a bit better than before, but by that I mean I was ordering healthier takeaways rather than living on Domino's. I needed to lose a couple of stone and I was out of shape, and this added to my paranoia about my life with Jess.

'James, I love you,' she said, time and time again. 'You're not a bad person. You're not the guy the media makes you out to be. You're not well. I know that. I know you. I understand your issues.'

After the tour, I moved out of the Hammersmith flat and into a flat in Chiswick. It was more like a family home and I thought it would suit me better than the penthouse flat, but it didn't. For some reason, I couldn't sleep upstairs and so I moved my bed down to the living room. I didn't know why, but I felt better down there. When I thought about why that was, I wondered if maybe I was trying to turn the clock back. I was happier on Mam's sofa than I was now. I was even happier on a park bench than I was now.

I began staying in the living room for days on end, smoking dope and watching TV. The news I'd been dropped from Syco was made public in June 2014. 'I think James, unfortunately, has had so many issues with what he has done publicly – which is a real issue with me,' Simon Cowell was quoted as saying. 'Somebody should have told him to shut up and just put the records out.'

My humiliation was complete, and my depression sank to a new low. I just wanted to curl up in a ball and die, and I had demons telling me I should end it all.

*Kill yourself, James. It's over. Your life is not worth living. There is no future for you, just a big, black space.*

I thought of my sisters, and I knew I couldn't do it. I had to be the man of the family. I couldn't do it to them, or to anyone else who loved me. I wanted to turn this around, but I didn't know if I could.

Caroline was still managing me for the time being, and she called to tell me a European promoter had been in touch, wanting to book me for a gig in Moldova. Despite being written off in the UK I had a loyal army of fans in Germany and Eastern Europe, and this was the only lifeline I had.

'I can't do it, no way.'

'But James, you can't say no. What else have you got? It's good money.'

'But I can't. You don't understand. I need to go into rehab, not get on a stage.'

The gig was worth several thousand pounds but money meant nothing to me. I'd lost track of how much – or how little – I had in the bank and I knew I was at breaking point mentally and needed help.

I'd started gambling over the previous six months or so. I thought I had unlimited funds and I kidded myself that gambling was a good distraction. It gave me a buzz I enjoyed when I was feeling low about all the things that were going wrong in my life, and it quickly became another addiction.

I set up an app on bet365 and began doing accumulator bets on football games and UFC boxing matches. I'd smash on £1,000 when I was stoned, convinced I could win. Then I'd lose it all and just think 'fuck it'. If I won I might blow £3,000 on another bet and lose the lot. I didn't care. My antidepressants numbed my emotions so much that I was prepared to take the hit just to feel the buzz, just to feel alive and to feel *something*, even just for the shortest time.

'James, you have £1,200 left in your bank account,' Caroline said.

'What do you mean? I thought I had loads of money . . .'

'James. Listen to me. That is all you have left. Your money is running out. You need to do this gig.'

My heart thumped. This was rock bottom. This was the absolute pits.

'I need to go to rehab. That's what I need to do.'

I hung up, and that is when I texted Jess, telling her exactly how I felt.

'I'm so sick. I'm giving up here. I'm losing my battle with depression. I'm crying. I've had enough. This is it. I'm not fighting. I need to go to rehab. I can't do it anymore. I'm sick. Babe, I'm crying. This is not me. All I can think about is curling into a ball. I hate myself. My mind is broken. I feel so sick. I'm scared of dying all the time. I'm permanently wired into my chest. I can't do it anymore. It has well and truly beaten me. I don't know what to do.'

Poor Jess. She was so scared when she got that message; she had lost someone she loved to suicide before, and she was genuinely scared I might take my own life. She kept a cool head, texting me back to keep up the dialogue as she dashed to the house.

'Since when has it been unbearable?'

'Since after we spoke last night. Since forever. I've always felt like this. I hate myself. I'm so sick. I want to collapse. I've finally realised I'm an addict. I'm tired of fighting it now. It's beaten me. I don't enjoy life anymore. I don't want to cope. I want to be happy. I want to be healthy.'

That last line was a breakthrough, though I didn't realise it at the time. I didn't want to die, not really. I wanted to mend myself. I wanted to come back from this, and I knew there was only one thing that could save me: my music.

# CHAPTER NINETEEN

*This is surreal. Is this really happening?*

'Rangers are shite!'

I was at my foster home, and in time I'd started to view my whole foster family as my real family. That's how I saw it. My foster mum had completely replaced Mam and would be there for me long term, no question. This was my family now.

One of the sons had never really liked me though, and he was always looking for ways to wind me up. He started having a go when we were watching Rangers play Manchester United on TV one day. He knew I was a surrogate Rangers fan because of my dad, and we were getting stuffed three–nil.

'What did I tell ya, Rangers are shite!'

'Leave it alone,' I snapped.

I was really pissed off because watching Rangers play always reminded me of my dad. I missed him. I was sixteen and had been in foster care for more than two years. It always upset me to think of Dad watching the game without me when we could have been watching it together.

'They are though. Rangers are shite!'

'Will you shut the fuck up and get out of my face?'

'Why should I? This is my house.'

This particular brother might have resented the fact I'd settled in so well and now viewed his family as my own. We started having a full-scale row. First, he said his mum and dad didn't really care about me, and then he told me they only took in foster kids for the money.

'You'll mean fuck all to any of us when you're gone,' he shouted.

The words cut me to the core and I lost my mind. I punched him, knocking him on his back, and when he picked himself up he went crying to his mum. Meanwhile I smarted even more than he did, despite the fact he hadn't hit me. My head and heart were aching. Maybe his mum didn't care about me at all? Had I been stupid to think she did, to think she might care enough to be there for me even when I was older?

After I threw that punch it was game over. I couldn't stay in my foster home any longer, and Social Services began urgent discussions about what to do with me. As I was already sixteen they couldn't very easily place me with another foster family, but there wasn't a council flat available for me either. The only answer was to offer me back to my family.

I waited about three weeks for news. It was unbearable in my foster home during that time because I felt that everybody hated me after what I'd done. Finally, I was told I was going back to live with Mam.

*Mam? My own mum? I thought she never wanted me back. Wow! Is this real?*

I had extremely mixed feelings. I couldn't wait to leave foster care but I was very afraid of what it would be like returning to Winchester Road. I hadn't seen Mam, Jazz or Neve for more than two years. Jazz was nine now and Neve was four. I'd missed a huge part of them growing up. I'd carried on seeing Dad very occasionally, and Sian, just around school, though we barely spoke. There is only one conversation I clearly remember having with Sian. One day I asked her if Mam ever talked about me. 'No James, not ever,' my sister replied.

I was told Mam was now with a new partner, a nice guy called Rob who lived in Hartlepool, and it seemed she was in a good place. Her depression was under control, and she was looking forward to having me back.

*This is surreal. Is this actually happening? It will probably go wrong. I know it will go wrong. But what choice do I have?*

Again, the fine details of my move have fallen into a mental black hole. I know I was confused and upset when I realised how naïve I'd been to think my foster mum had become my real mum. That was painful, but I was also relieved to get out of her house after what had gone on. I have no memories of saying goodbye to my foster mum, or of any emotional reunion with Mam and my little sisters. Suddenly I was back in Winchester Road. It was honestly like I'd been in a time warp; it was that weird.

'Rob, this is my son James,' Mam said proudly. 'He's got the most amazing voice and he writes his own songs and plays the acoustic guitar.'

'Pleased to meet you. I've heard a lot about you and I'm really looking forward to hearing you sing.'

Mam didn't want to talk about foster care and it was as if the past few years had never happened. She spoke as if I was her blue-eyed boy who'd just been away on a school trip or something like that. It was so odd. She was like a completely different person to the one I remembered, sitting around that table in the Social Services office and saying she wanted nothing more to do with me.

I played by her rules, because I knew better than to cross my mum, and I liked this version of her. This was my real mum, the one who sang with me in the kitchen when I was a little boy, the one who applauded me like I was a superstar when I was on stage in Bahrain. I was happy to let her sweep the past under the carpet, because I was just very grateful to be back there, welcomed into the family once again.

Right from the start of being back at home, Mam encouraged me with my music. I never had a pen and notepad out of my hand and lyrics were pouring out of me. Once I sat all day writing a song called 'Today'. It contained the line, 'Sisters and brothers, look out for each other, at the end of the day, don't be afraid to say I love you.'

'I've written this song, Mam, and I think it's really special.'

'Can you play it for me then, James? I'd love to hear it.'

I felt awkward. We had double French doors between our two living rooms in the house, and I asked Mam if she could sit on one side and I'd go on the other. She agreed, and then I picked up my guitar and performed my song, with Mam listening through the glass.

'That is *amazing*!' Mam shouted. 'That is such a special song! It's a universal anthem. I think that will really touch people. Well done, James!'

Mam was absolutely buzzing. This was a pivotal moment for me, because Mam's reaction made me realise for the first time how powerful songwriting can be. My music could touch people. I could communicate with others through my music, and it might even help them. This was mind-blowing, because up until now I'd been very self-indulgent with my songwriting. Everything I wrote was for me, as a way of working through my feelings, but now I wanted to touch other people with my music.

Mam started to help me record my songs onto a hard drive. She had a £5 mic and a very basic sound recorder on her computer, and when you pressed the space bar you got one minute at a time to record. Mam would sit there for hours, helping me get my music down.

'Mam, press it again,' I'd say.

'OK. Go on son, do it!'

We went on to record hundreds of songs like that. Mam could see how much I loved my music, and she enjoyed being a part of it and was very willing and patient. It was an incredibly bonding time for us. One song, 'Simmer', was about the demons in my head and the fights I had in my mind, between the good thoughts and the bad thoughts. Mam listened to every lyric. It must have been very painful for her to hear my innermost thoughts, but we still didn't discuss my time in foster care, or any other problems of the past. I guess Mam had decided that helping me get my words out like this was the best way to help me cope and move forward.

Most weekends Mam would disappear off to Hartlepool to see Rob, taking Jasmin and Neve with her. I'd have free run of the house because Sian was always doing her own thing, and I threw some legendary parties for my friends. For a while, going to 'Raff's house' became the big thing to do at the weekend. The house would be packed with what felt like every teenager from Redcar and I'd have buckets of booze in the bath. It was wild, so much so that on one memorable night the police turned up and started arresting a couple of guys outside.

'What's going on?' I asked, watching as the lads I didn't recognise were handcuffed and bundled into a police car.

'They're Redcar's most wanted,' came the deadly serious reply.

I laughed. I was having a great time and I didn't care about any consequences. Deep down I guess I reckon I knew it was only a matter of time before my relationship with Mam would relapse again. I'd probably be out on my arse next week, so I made the most of having the house to myself and having some fun. Mam never seemed to mind; she was happy with Rob.

After I left school I enrolled on a BTEC national diploma in music performance, at a college in Middlesbrough. I had no idea what else to do and one of my mates from school, Nathan Futo, was doing the course and told me about it. Right from the start I didn't really like it there. The teachers seemed to be bitter, failed musicians who didn't really care, and they'd turn up late and criticise us instead of encouraging us.

All the kids on the course were put into bands at the start of term, and the idea was that you created music together and performed it for your end-of-year assessment. I didn't gel with the group I was put with, but I did hit it off with a few other lads and so eventually five of us decided to break away and form our own band. There was Nathan, Beanie, Col and Cad, and we formed an indie band together called Traceless. We liked Arctic Monkeys and Razorlight and we had Oasis and Libertines vibes going on. I loved it; the rest of the course didn't interest me at all, but playing in a band was very cool and we practised as much as we could.

We got our first gig at the Ku Bar in Stockton. I was still only sixteen, going on seventeen, and I was really nervy. My hair was super-long and I had it pulled over my right eye as I was still so paranoid about how I looked. It was only when I started to perform that I found my confidence, just like I had when I got on stage as a kid. My voice was raw and powerful; I was the singer with the attitude and I'd just go mental, swinging the mic and trying to be Alex Turner, Johnny Borrell or Pete Doherty. I was still learning guitar, so I'd also stand with my hands behind my back like Liam Gallagher, dressed in one of those military-style coats with brass buttons and red piping. Nathan played guitar and we'd joke that he was Noel to my Liam. It was fun, and for a while I was never happier than when I was with Traceless.

We put a cover set together and word went around Redcar that we could do Oasis and The Jam really well, and then we started to get booked for lots of gigs in local pubs, earning about £20 or £30 each a night. We also put some music out online, on MySpace, and received quite a lot of local support that way too. I really enjoyed it, but then something happened that made me even happier. Her name was Jenna, and she completely turned my head.

'Why weren't you at college today?' one of the lads asked. 'We were hoping to do a bit of band practice.'

'Oh, I was just with Jenna . . .'

She was my first proper girlfriend and I fell head over heels in love with her. Overnight, all I wanted to do was hang out with Jenna and I started to lose interest in going to college. I couldn't see the point. I already had a band and my confidence in my musical ability was solid and growing all the time. I knew I was going to make it as a singer, so why was I bothering with the course? 'You're never gonna be the next Oasis you know,' a teacher had said to us one day. That summed it up; they'd lost me from that moment on.

I dropped out of college after the first year, which upset a lot of people. The lads thought I was an arsehole for quitting. Traceless fell apart, and Mam was furious with me. She'd been so proud of me and had been telling everyone how well I was doing on the course and with the band, and she was worried about my future.

'You have to stick at things, James,' she said. 'You have a talent. Why are you throwing this opportunity away? You can choose the good path in life or the bad path. You need to start choosing the good one.'

This was something Mam had said to me before, when I was a boy and had been in trouble at school. I can remember her sitting on my bunk bed, looking serious. I didn't listen to her then and I wasn't listening now, because I didn't believe for one minute that staying in college was my passport to the future.

'I'll make it anyway, Mam. The course is shit. I don't need it.'

The atmosphere in the house soured after that. We'd relapsed in our relationship, Mam and me, just like I always knew we would, although while she was with Rob things never got really bad. She was still in a happy place in her personal life, and that definitely went in my favour. Mam wasn't throwing me out again or hurling accusations and hurtful comments at me, although she was on my case all the time, asking when I was ever going to sort myself out. Essentially, Mam recognised way before I did that it was during the times in my life when I wasn't fully occupied that I slipped into trouble.

*Avoid the spaces in between.*

Mam encouraged me to accept support that was available through Social Services. She could see I needed guidance and help and I wasn't listening to her. I reluctantly agreed, and it was a good decision. I was assigned a support worker who was part of a mentor programme set up to help kids like me. He was brilliant. I saw him at a place called The Junction on Queen Street in Redcar and he helped me with practical stuff, like showing me how to apply for a passport and my provisional driving licence. It was good to have someone to talk to who had no preconceived ideas about me and was focused purely on helping me. He also sorted out stuff like benefits and getting me registered at the Job Centre, but most of all he was a guy I could drop in on whenever I wanted to, and someone I could be honest with without the fear of being judged or shouted at. I told him I wasn't interested in getting a regular job because music was the only thing I wanted to do and he listened and didn't patronise me. I respected him for that and paid attention to all the other stuff he guided me through.

By now friends were starting to say to me, 'Why don't you go on *Pop Idol*?' I'd tell them firmly I didn't want to go down that route. I believed in my music. I believed I was good. And because I had so much confidence in my musical ability I believed very strongly I could make it on my own. I didn't need *Pop Idol*, just like I didn't need college, or Traceless.

I spent my days with Jenna and had no routine whatsoever. I became a real Emo, writing songs about my life and all the pain and trauma I'd gone through. Inevitably, I got under Mam's feet and the regular blow-ups we had about my lifestyle and my attitude began to get brutal. Just like when I was little, I started to be wary of her moods and I was watchful of them, because I knew her mood could change the course of my day.

'James, you're so lazy! You're useless – just like your dad.'

*Here we go. She's having a bad day. Not this again.*

I'd try to stay out of her way as much as I could when I saw the signs. It was a rerun of when I was a boy, except instead of going out to play football at every opportunity I was shutting myself away with my music, or with my girlfriend.

'Don't start, Mam, please!'

'Why do you have to be so aggressive? Why are you so angry? You're scaring your sisters with all your shouting, James. Stop it!'

Whenever the old criticisms and accusations were wheeled out I couldn't for the life of me work out why, because I never started out being angry and aggressive.

'Mam, can't you just leave me alone? You're causing trouble out of nothing.'

'Be quiet, James. All I ever hear is the worst word from your mouth. Come on girls! Just ignore him when he's in this mood!'

'Mam, how can you say that? *You* started having a go at *me* for no reason and I haven't even said anything!'

It was so frustrating and I could feel myself slipping back in time, to the dark days before I went into foster care. It was all girls together in the house, all over again. Big bad James had come back and upset the applecart. It was like Mam had been programmed never to move on from the past, and always to use me as her scapegoat.

My songs got more Emo the more I fell out with Mam. She started kicking me out again, and a few times I snuck back and slept in the garage without her knowing. It was cold and dusty and full of junk, but whenever I slept in there I felt better. I had my own space. I could lock the door. It was better than sleeping on Mam's sofa in the back room, which was where I usually slept as the girls had the beds.

'Why don't you just let me move into the garage?' I suggested eventually. 'It'll be better for everyone.'

Mam agreed; I think she was relieved. I cleared out the junk and the spiders and painted the breezeblock bricks of the garage walls in a burnt pink. I also tried to insulate it myself, but it was still always freezing cold. I didn't really care; it was a place I could go and play and write music to my heart's content, away from the pressures and unpredictable atmosphere in the house.

'D'you fancy joining another band?'

It was my mate Nathan. He'd had formed another group along with a new wave of guys who'd joined college after I left.

'I'll come and meet them, why not?'

I'd done all right on my own for a while after Traceless and had even put out some of my own stuff on MySpace and picked up some local support, but I was interested in this new band. There was a guy called Jordan Swain on drums who

was absolutely phenomenal – he is now one of the top drum-
mers in the UK – and another guy called Vinnie who was an
incredible musician, along with Cov from Traceless plus
Nathan. The band was called Moonlight Drive. They were
into soulful rock and Pearl Jam – it was like The Doors meets
Incubus – and I was impressed. I joined the band and loved it,
and when Nathan subsequently left I became lead guitar as
well as the frontman.

Moonlight Drive lasted about a year before we broke up
due to what can only be called 'creative differences'. It sounds
a bit laughable to say that about a bunch of teenage lads but
that was the truth. Me and Vinnie were Emos. We were into
pop-punk and wanted to be Blink-182, but Jordan and Cov
didn't really like that vibe. Nevertheless, it was good while it
lasted. We used to make about £150 a night in local pubs
doing a cover set, and we put our own recordings out on
MySpace. It was an eclectic mix and the musicianship had
improved since Traceless. We made a few waves and picked up
some fans and followers, and I really thought I was finally
going places, and that it would only be a matter of time before
a big opportunity came along. After the band broke up I still
felt the same. Whether I was in a band or on my own, I was
going to make it, no question about it.

I was on my own in another sense now too. Jenna dumped
me after we'd been together for a year. It came out of the blue
and completely broke my heart. I never really knew what went
wrong. I know she didn't like the drama at my house and the
way I was living in the garage and arguing with Mam, but I
never really got an explanation. To this day, she's the only girl
who's properly broken my heart, because after Jenna, I vowed I
would never get that deep again. I'd totally immersed myself in

the relationship, and when we split up I was left feeling bruised and vulnerable. I was all alone in the world; that's how I felt.

One day Michael Dawson, who still lived down the road, invited me over to his house, just as he had done in the past. He introduced me to his mates Danny McCauley and Michael Petite and straight away I felt a connection to them. None of us had our dads around and we were all out of work and drifting along. There was Jamie Graham too, although he wasn't in the same boat as the rest of us, as he had a very good life and lived with both his parents.

Petite had a reputation for being even harder than Dawson and I liked the way these lads stood for no shit. They didn't go looking for trouble, and you knew that once you were friends they'd always have your back. I could say anything to them: all four are my very best friends to this day.

The lads had an open-minded attitude I admired, especially when it came to music. They were all into heavy rock but appreciated lots of different kinds of music. Jamie and me, especially, connected through music. We'd both slag off shit manufactured pop acts and complain about the public being tricked into buying their music. We wanted to be the antidote to crap like that.

Dawson loved the fact I could sing and play the guitar and he really championed me, telling the others how he'd first heard me sing years earlier.

'Sing "Red Eyes",' Dawson said one day when I was at his mam's house.

I felt shy and awkward, even though Dawson was bigging me up as he always did.

'Listen to this,' he said to the others, explaining this was one of the songs I wrote myself. 'He's unbelievable.'

'OK, but can you turn the lights out?'

That's how it went. In an intimate situation like this I could perform so much better in the dark, when there was no danger I might have to look someone in the eye. It was just like hiding behind the French doors when I performed for Mam.

*You're not good enough. People might laugh. Don't look them in the eye, because then you won't see if they are laughing at you.*

'Mate, that was amazing. You're brilliant!'

All the lads were joining in, piling on the praise, drowning out the demons.

I felt good. I only ever felt normal when I was in my music, and I only ever felt truly happy when I was connecting with people through my music. There was no doubt in my mind. Even though I had no clue how my career was going to take off, I had faith that it would, any time soon.

# CHAPTER TWENTY

*This isn't right. I'm not dead. The X Factor is not going to define me*

'Can I come and play football?'

'Yes mate, be good to have you. We play on a Wednesday night.'

'Great. I'm really looking forward to it.'

It was a relief to have a normal conversation about something so regular. After I'd been dropped by Syco and hit rock bottom I had a kind of awakening. I didn't want to die. I wanted to be happy and healthy; that's what I'd ended my texts with, after I shared my darkest, innermost thoughts with Jess. I was tired of the way I was living my life. I was sick to death of feeling depressed and I was exhausted by my panic attacks. I didn't want my life to be like this any more. I had to change it.

I began reading some self-help books and with Jess's help I forced myself to think positively, about what would make me happy. Football was the first thing that came to mind. I've always genuinely loved football, and having a regular game really appealed to me.

The team I joined was with a group of lads in Chiswick and I absolutely loved it. The guys didn't recognise me from *The X Factor*, or if they did they didn't say anything. It was so liberating. I could have been a boy again, kicking a ball around Winchester Road, using my little green anorak as a goalpost.

*Nothing's changed. You're still a misfit. These lads think you're weird.*

*SHUT UP. It's not true. They don't know me. They're not judging me. I'm not that guy who won* The X Factor *and threw it all away. I AM NOT LISTENING TO YOU.*

My own voice was winning out more and more against the demons, although I did have a setback on one of those footy nights. A man hammered on my car window when I was in traffic, and I wound the window down, wondering what the problem was.

'Are you that guy who won *The X Factor*? What are you doing now, mate?'

The guy was staring at me like I was some kind of strange exhibit, and I was taken aback. What did he think I was doing? Did this stranger think I wasn't making music any more, just because I wasn't on his TV? Did he think I'd lost my voice because I lost my record deal? I could feel myself crumble and I began to struggle to breathe.

*He thinks you died. He thinks you should be dead on the floor. You can't be alive if you're not on TV or if you don't have a record deal. Face it, James, you are as good as dead.*

*No. This isn't right. I'm not dead.* The X Factor *is not going to define me. I have to prove I can do it all again, on my own.*

The experience really bothered me, but it also sparked a flash of determination. I had to make more music. I had to make a comeback. I had to prove that I didn't just have a hit record because I was on *The X Factor*, and I had to show the world that I wasn't some washed-up has-been.

When the new series of *The X Factor* started, I steeled myself to watch. As soon as I saw the opening titles I began to gasp for breath. It triggered a lot of stress as it took me right back to being immersed in the chaos backstage and struggling to perform below par when I was drugged up on prescription pills. It also provoked feelings of anger and abject disappointment, because in this new series, in 2014, I was not mentioned at all. They announced they were looking for the next Leona Lewis, Olly Murs or One Direction, but there was no mention of me. I'd had the biggest-selling *X Factor* single in the show's history but now I'd been deleted. It was like I'd never existed; no wonder people wondered what the hell had become of me.

'What the fuck . . . ? This is my legacy and they're not respecting it. I can't deal with this. Did it really happen? What was it all for?'

I couldn't breathe at all.

*You might as well be dead, James. This show is the only thing that confirms your existence. You don't exist any more. Your life is over.*

'Turn it off, please,' I gasped.

I had to get Jess to call an ambulance that night because I had a really bad panic attack. The paramedic who turned up was very kind and understanding. He asked me if I'd been smoking weed, which I had, and he told me he used to smoke a bit when he was younger. Then he advised me to have it pure, without tobacco.

'The chemicals in the tobacco are causing an adrenaline dump,' he explained. 'The nicotine is putting you in "fight or flight" mode. Do you know what I mean?'

I did, very well. I felt like that as a boy, when I was on hyper-alert, watching and waiting to see what Mam would do next.

'Man, I know exactly what you mean,' I said. I had a vivid image of walking home from school, avoiding the cracks in the pavement, then opening the front door with fear and trep-idation, scared that Mam might be in a bad mood.

'OK. Well if you're gonna smoke, do it without tobacco my friend. I think it'll help with your anxiety.'

As the paramedic had been so cool and helpful I asked if I could have his number, and he and his colleague agreed to set up a WhatsApp chat group for the three of us. I knew I needed professional intervention in order to calm down from a panic attack and I hoped that just having this group to hand would help me. It did. I messaged the guys countless times after that, and thanks to them I called out fewer and fewer ambulances.

I couldn't get over being deleted from the X Factor history and it really ate away at me. I had a lot of anger, but I knew I had to channel my energy in a positive way. It was the only way forward; I couldn't change the past, but what I did in the here and now was in my control. This was one of the things I'd learned from reading self-help books, and in particular

*The Power of Now* by Eckhart Tolle. Being in the now was my power. I was in charge of my present, and if I got things right now it would have a positive influence on my future.

At the end of December I attended a 'Women of the Year' award ceremony in London. I bumped into Simon Cowell's brother Tony, who I'd been introduced to before and he'd always been a huge support. When he asked me how I was I decided to take the bull by the horns.

'I'm massively disappointed with everything that's happened,' I told him. 'I still can't believe I've been dropped by Syco and I really want them to give me a second chance. I feel it's the only way back for me. I'm on a much better path now. Can you tell Simon what I've said?'

Tony listened and nodded, and said he could do better than that.

'I'll ask Simon to call tonight,' he said.

Simon was in the US and I waited up. We'd met briefly a couple of times before, once when I had to pose for a photo with him a few months after I won the show and once in his dressing room. I wasn't at ease on either occasion, but someone told me Simon liked confident people, and that when Cher Lloyd went in to see him she put her feet up on his table and sparked up a cigarette, which he liked. It meant that when I met Simon for the first time I took the cigarette he offered and told myself to look confident, but I was overthinking everything because of my nerves. I started shaking and suddenly forgot how to smoke, and then I took the most awkward, self-conscious drag, not knowing how to inhale or even hold the cigarette. I cringed at the memory, but now there was no room for nerves. Two years had passed, and I'd been in the wilderness for long enough. Simon was phoning me from America, and it was time to step up and make myself heard. This was the opportunity I needed, and I was fighting for my life.

When my mobile finally rang at 3 a.m. I gripped it and told myself to breathe steadily. Simon sounded cheerful and ready to listen so I just went for it.

'The way I see it,' I told him, 'is there's no point in me winning *The X Factor* if I'm not the best thing to come from it.'

'I love that attitude, James.'

I could picture Simon smiling and nodding, and so I ploughed on.

'If I'm done now, and it's because of my behaviour and not my music, I can't have that, Simon. I cannot accept that my career is over, and I believe the only way I can get back on track is with your help.'

Simon listened and then started to ask me about normal stuff, like where I was living and how I was feeling. I think he was trying to suss out if I was crazy or not. I wanted to be honest and I talked openly about the issues I had at that time.

Simon said he wanted to work with me again but said it was not just down to him. Sonny Takhar was the head of Syco, and he and his whole team would have to agree to take me back on. I thanked Simon and told him I understood. It had been a very good call, and I felt hopeful, despite the fact Simon had made no promises.

I pictured myself going back on *The X Factor* when I'd made my comeback, and I wanted that more than anything else in the world. Simon's call energised me. I visualised myself on the stage and I was prepared to do anything to make that comeback happen.

Now I was looking for every way possible to get myself out of the hole I'd put myself in. Playing football helped massively in opening my eyes to what I needed to do. I wanted to get fitter, as I was struggling a bit on the pitch, and it became very obvious what I had to do.

'I'm getting my life together,' I told Jess. 'This is it. I'm coming off everything – the pills, the weed, the lot.'

Jess was relieved as she'd been wanting me to do this for a long time. She comes from a family of medical professionals, and Jess had a lot of practical advice to share about good nutrition and exercise, and how both could help me get better. She had my back and I was so grateful to her; she was my only friend in London.

I quit smoking weed and came off everything overnight. I knew it wasn't the best or the easiest way to do it, but I was so done with it all, and once I'd made my mind up I just couldn't wait.

'I don't care how hard it is,' I told Jess. 'I'm doing it. This starts today.'

I knew it was going to be hell, and it was worse than that. It was like being in a coma for days and days afterwards. There were big blank spots blotting my mind and my memory. I felt fragile and jittery and vulnerable and paranoid, but I kept going, with Jess's help.

'How do you feel?' she asked every time I woke up, and she became a sounding board for so many irrational, nonsensical thoughts and ideas.

I started off saying I felt like I'd been in a train crash. I obsessed about whether I might be truly mad. Did I have schizophrenia? Should Mam have taken me for that MRI scan all those years ago? Should I take myself for one now?

Did I need psychiatric help? I was wary of going down that route and I still am. I Googled all kinds of scary stuff about all the drugs I'd taken in the past and their possible side effects. Had I killed off some brain cells with weed? Had I given myself psychosis with drugs? Was this detox too little, too late?

Eventually I had a breakthrough. One day, when Jess asked me how I was feeling, I had a very lucid thought.

'I feel closer to my mind,' I said. I can't tell you how good it felt to say that.

I was writing a lot of music and my notebook was littered with lyrics. 'The Truth' was the first song I wrote after I lost my deal. It's the most autobiographical of all the tracks that eventually ended up on my album, and contains my favourite line of all: 'the comedown's harder in the headlines.' Writing it was a cathartic experience. I was forming ideas for so many more songs, like 'Back from the Edge' and 'Train Wreck'. It was my therapy, and I knew I had to tell the story of my demise and my comeback through my songs.

I moved out of the Chiswick flat and into a light and airy top-floor flat not far away, near some water. I wanted a fresh start and to feel I could breathe more easily. I instantly felt happier in my new flat and I kitted it out with some gym equipment and a recording desk. I even got two kittens, Bambino and Archibald, aka Bambi and Archie. I had two dogs for a short time – Smokey and Biggie – but to be honest I'd got them during a very spontaneous stoned moment, when I was trying to find fulfilment. The dogs couldn't stay, but now I was finally looking after myself I felt able to look after other living creatures, and I liked having the cats mooching around.

I spent hours writing music and I was prolific. I knew, without a doubt, that I could only fully recover when I got recognition for my music. It wasn't always therapeutic; a lot of the time it was the opposite. I felt like a prisoner in my own head, because I was working through so much pain and trauma of the past.

The flat has a balcony, and whenever I had a panic attack, which was still happening all the time, I'd go out to try to help my breathing. I'd take in as much air as I could, and I'd look over the edge.

*Just do it. Why are you suffering? You can't even breathe properly, James. You could end it now.*

*No! Step back from the edge. You can't do this, James.*

I'd see myself falling off my balcony and see my dead body on the ground, and there were many times when I felt so close to going over. Thinking about my sisters stopped me. I thought of all my siblings, and Mam and Dad, as well as Jess and my best mates from home. I saw their faces, imagined them, very clearly, standing by my grave, shedding tears, feeling guilty, wishing they had been able to stop me. No way. There was no way I could do that to the people I loved.

I was going to stay alive, and I had to support myself. Everything came back to my music, and the words and the songs began to flow out of me more and more. I wanted to make an album I would be so proud of, and I was happy I could be completely myself this time round. It was going to be very tough to claw my way back without a record deal, but it wasn't impossible.

Impossible. That word again, that song. Even though nobody in the industry in Britain wanted to know about me, I was starting to get a lot of calls about gigs in Europe. The promoter was a guy called George, who was based in Moldova.

'You have a massive fan base here,' George said. 'I can book you for lots of gigs, James. They want you to sing "Impossible". That's what they know you for. They love you.'

He wanted to book me for one-off concerts and nightclub gigs, personal appearances and even some big festivals in places like Bulgaria, Romania, Portugal, the Balearics, Poland and Germany.

This wasn't exactly my dream but I was very grateful to George. I had no choice. I had no money coming in and I was racking up debts. The gigs paid well, but the fact I needed them so much rattled me to the core. What if this was all that was left for me? Would I be a one-hit wonder, that guy who hawked the same song all over Europe year after year? I was only twenty-six years old; the thought was soul-destroying, and the reality was even worse.

I started flying out to do gigs all over Europe, most week-ends, which sounds a lot more glamorous than it is. It would usually be a question of travelling with just enough time to prepare for the gig, performing at what was the equivalent of the early hours of the morning for me, then coming straight back later that day. It was exhausting, I got no time to enjoy the countries and I could have been anywhere, really, as I'd just be in and out of airports and venues and hotels.

At one performance – I've no idea where – my whole neuro-logical system felt like it was electrocuting me and I started having a panic attack on stage.

*Breathe, James. Keep breathing. You can't have a panic attack on stage.*

I was in the middle of 'Impossible' and I just held the mic out to the audience and got them to sing while I stood there dragging as much air as I could into my lungs, clinging on to as much control as I could. It was a hideous experience, like I was having an internal panic attack.

I hated staying in hotel rooms on my own. They reminded me of my time on *The X Factor*, and what I'd lost. One time it felt like my skin started to crawl when I walked in the room on my own. I couldn't breathe.

On another occasion, I was doing a festival in Poland and some of the organisers offered to take me and the boys in the band to a club. When we got there, it was a tacky strip joint and one of the girls tried to drag me off. I wasn't interested, and when I started to protest one of the owners of the club got really angry with me.

'I'm sorry, mate, but I'm not attracted to her,' I made the mistake of saying.

I took a punch on my nose and then on the side of my face. Suddenly there were four guys on me and I was manhandled out of the club. I went berserk and forced my way back inside as I'd lost the lads, and then I ended up getting properly beaten up. My nose had never been straight after scraps I'd had at school, but now it was battered completely out of shape. We laugh about it now but at the time it was a pretty unedifying experience; there had to be more to my career and my life than this.

I was finally thrown a lifeline after I bumped into Russell Eslamifar in London. I'd just had laser eye surgery and I joked that I wasn't being a diva wearing sunglasses indoors. Russell laughed and said he knew I was no diva. When he looked after publicity on *The X Factor*, Russell was the one who always got me out of photo shoots and random events he knew I wouldn't want to do. 'It's just not James, don't even ask him,' he'd say, because he totally got me.

Russell told me he was planning to move into talent management, and he explained that what he'd witnessed happening to my career was his driving force. He wished he had been in a position to help me when I was destroying myself on Twitter, and he told me he wanted to stop that happening to other artists. I was quite taken aback and touched by this, plus I knew Russell had always rated me. We agreed to have a proper catch-up when the time was right.

Russell called me a few months later, when he had made his move and joined James Grant Management. It was the summer of 2015, and I was feeling fitter, both mentally and physically. By now I'd finally parted company with my old management. We'd run our course together and I had no regrets, but it meant I was completely alone professionally. I'd written loads of music for my next album and was proud of what I'd produced, but I was at the point where I knew I needed help and guidance to push things forward. My reputation was still in the gutter in the UK, even after all this time, and I didn't know if any other management would touch me.

'When I heard you'd been dropped by Syco I was devastated,' Russell said. 'I always believed you were the biggest talent to ever come from *The X Factor*.' He was very angry about the way I'd been left to self-destruct, as it looked to us, although we both conceded I'd probably become unmanageable by the time I did all that damage on Twitter.

Russell listened to my new music and asked how I would feel about him bringing me into James Grant. I knew the company looked after amazing artists like The Script and the Manic Street Preachers and I jumped at the opportunity.

'That would be perfect,' I said. Yes! This could be it. This could be the turning point for me. I was very grateful; it was the only real lifeline I'd had in a very long time.

Russell explained that he couldn't make any promises and that he had to sell the idea to his bosses, Neil Rodford and Martin Hall. Even then we'd have a long way to go. 'But let me take that risk,' he said. 'Let me try to bring you in.'

I had a meeting with Neil and Martin and it went very well. I was completely honest with them about everything that had gone on and where I was now. They appreciated my honesty and liked the new music I'd written, and I liked them a lot. They are both straightforward, real guys and we all knew exactly where we stood. This was a long shot; I was still up-river and there was no guarantee my career could ever be rescued, but we agreed to pull together and try our best.

After that meeting, I started to believe my story might truly be able to come full circle. It could be rags to riches, all over again. Maybe I really could come back.

That night I stood on the balcony of my flat and thought about the major crossroads I'd been at in my life before. Bahrain. Coming home. Going into foster care. That was the biggest one of the lot. *Will you have your son for half the week?* Going to the *X Factor* audition. *What have you got to lose?* I had nothing to lose then, nothing at all. Then over-night I had it all. I had everything to lose, and I lost *everything*. But that was not the end of my story. I felt that very strongly. I believed I could make a comeback, and I wanted it so much.

I looked down to the paving stones below and instead of thinking about falling to the ground as I had done so many times, I looked up to the sky. Then I thought about a line I'd written for the title track of my album, *Back from the Edge*.

*Back to the boy who would reach for the stars.*

I wondered if I could be him again. Could I go back to the boy who would reach for the stars? I felt I could. I was a boy again, a boy with a dream. And I was going to do everything I could to make it come true.

# CHAPTER TWENTY-ONE

## That is the life you're meant to have, James

'I want to declare myself homeless.'

I was eighteen years old and Mam had thrown me out one last time. I wasn't welcome to stay in the garage, because we'd got into a destructive cycle that neither of us could tolerate any longer.

From my point of view, it had become like living with two different people again. As ever, when Mam was in a good mood, she told me how proud she was of my music and filled me with confidence about the future. She'd started pulling out all the stops to help me be heard outside the local pub circuit, where I was still performing covers on my own. Mam sent demo tapes of my music to loads of radio stations and begged DJs all the time, 'Just give my son a listen.' Some responded and I got a bit of airplay on online radio shows and was introduced to a few contacts, though ultimately nothing ever came of it. 'It'll happen, darlin',' Mam always told me. 'You have to be patient. You're so talented and there's no way a talent like yours can go unnoticed.'

On a bad day, Mam would rip me to shreds, flipping out and telling me I shouldn't be doing gigs for £100 in a pub. 'What are you doing with your life? You're wasting your talent, James. Why don't you sort yourself out and stop doing these dead-end gigs?' It cut me deep every time when she criticised me, and I'd retaliate by shouting back, telling her to keep her nose out and accusing her of having issues and being out of control.

'I'm the one with issues? You're the one who needs to get a grip, James. You can't spend the rest of your life playing your guitar in the garage and sleeping in until the afternoon, you know. You'll make nothing of yourself, just like your father.'

That was the rub of it, and in the end, I couldn't stand it at home any more than Mam could stand having me there.

'Get out!' she screamed dramatically, after one final argument. 'I've had enough of you! You can get out and you can stay out this time. You're not welcome here.'

*Brilliant. Just wash your hands of me all over again. Pretend I don't exist. You don't even have to sign the papers to get rid of me this time.*

I spent a few nights staying at Dawson's. We'd become really good mates over the past year or so and his mum was really cool and didn't mind me staying on her sofa, but I didn't want to put them out. I couldn't bear the thought that Dawson might see me as a loser or a burden. He lent me a sleeping bag, and I started to take it out with me so I could sleep rough, staying on park benches like I had before. I don't think I admitted what I was doing to Dawson; it was so embarrassing, and I didn't want to talk about it.

I lost count of the number of trips I made into town to beg the council to give me a place to live. I'd been on the list for a council house for ages. I was desperate now, but I never seemed to move up the list. In the end, it was my mentor from the buddy programme I'd been on at The Junction who advised me to declare myself officially homeless – which I was – and it worked. A few weeks later I was given emergency accommodation in a local B&B.

I moved in with a couple of carrier bags of belongings, and I felt so alone and fearful it was untrue. The place was like a hostel for ex-cons and was as rough as anything. My room was small and grim, with a dirty, stained carpet, threadbare curtains and peeling wallpaper. I had to share a stinking toilet and mouldy bathroom with loads of other men, and after a breakfast of a rubber egg and a greasy sausage I was shown the door every morning, and told I was not allowed to return until the evening.

I'd go around to Mam's sometimes, because I didn't know what else to do with myself. I wasn't eating properly and I'd always tell her I was hungry. I was receiving benefits of £87 a fortnight and it was a struggle to survive, especially as I had no way of cooking for myself and had no idea how to budget.

'Get your dad to feed you,' she'd shout. 'It's his turn to sort you out. I've looked after you for long enough. I've done my bit. I'm done!'

I did what I'd done before and shoplifted from the local supermarkets when I got hungry. I'd always feel a rush of exhilaration when I got away with it and I'd tear into the food, but afterwards guilt and shame crept in.

*Look at you, James. Nobody wants you. Nobody cares. What is your life? You're the lowest of the low, man.*

I spent a really tough six weeks in the B&B before I was given a flat on Lumley Road in Redcar. When I heard I was getting a place of my own I thought it was fantastic, but the reality was the flat was an absolute dump. It was freezing cold and damp and the kitchen had mould growing up the walls. I was sick from the day I moved in, coughing and spluttering because I always felt the damp on my chest. The landlord wasn't interested when I complained and so I just had to make do, but at least I had my own place, and it was somewhere me and my mates could hang out.

Dawson, Danny and Petite came around all the time. Every one of us was batshit poor, and we began knocking around together every day, feeling like outcasts and outlaws.

'I've got you this, mate,' Dawson would say, presenting me with bags of food from his mum's cupboards. I'd lost weight and was painfully thin, to the point where I looked almost anorexic. I was always so grateful for anything he or the other lads brought round.

There was nothing in the flat and most days we'd just walk the streets, kicking a ball and hanging around. Sometimes we'd go into the 24-hour Tesco, and I'd smash open the cases on the video games so the security tag wouldn't go off and then walk out with the latest FIFA game for the PlayStation. I loved the fact we were beating the system, it felt amazing.

Stealing food was ridiculously easy too, as the security in the local supermarkets was so lackadaisical. I would take in empty carrier bags and cruise the aisles, helping myself to crisps and chocolate bars and Pot Noodles. When the carrier bags were full I'd just walk out brazenly, straight past the tills.

'What have we got?' I'd say, laughing as I rummaged through the haul. I still felt horrible about myself for doing this, but what could I do? It was a basic survival tactic and if I didn't steal my food I'd have hunger pains and headaches.

At night, after Tesco's shut, we'd play football in the car park, often with another mate called Alex who was also on the dole. We played a game called 'booty' where the loser of a game would stand against the wall and everyone else would have a turn of kicking the ball at them. One night we had a bit more excitement than that, when we broke into a friend's house, at his request. The lad had been kicked out by his mum and wanted his computer back, so he recruited us to help him retrieve it. We didn't think twice; we thought we were like Robin Hood's Merry Men, robbing the rich to help the poor.

On Thursdays, we'd go to the indie night in the local pub. It was £1 a pint and we'd get absolutely smashed on less than a tenner and all pile back to Lumley Road. Occasionally we'd smoke a bit of weed if one of the lads brought it round, but it wasn't a big part of my life, not then.

I was still doing a few gigs and putting some music out online, on MySpace mostly, but I'd become half-hearted with it. A few of the fans I'd picked up locally were quite hardcore and my name was well known around the town, but I wasn't putting as much effort into my music as I had when I was still living at home. I was lazy, I'd lost my way and I had other things on my mind now I was living on my own. Deep down I still thought I'd make it one day, come what may, because I never lost faith in my ability. That was the one thing I kept a grip on, always.

I only went looking for gigs when I was really desperate for money. Then I'd put ten covers together, go to the local pub and blag myself a one-hour set. It always went down well, I'd get a buzz from it, and often I'd celebrate by buying beers for the boys, or getting everyone a takeaway. Then I'd be skint all over again. I was so clueless when it came to money. I had a £50 overdraft facility at the bank, and when I got my £87 benefits paid every fortnight I'd often withdraw £137, spend about £100 in the first week and be left with £30 to live on for the second week. There were many occasions when I had to sell a guitar I'd saved up for to the local music shop, to pay my rent. Then I couldn't write songs and I hated that.

I eventually got kicked out of Lumley Road, for being too noisy, and I was rehoused in a bedsit on the seafront in Saltburn, six miles from Redcar. Even though the two towns aren't far apart they have very different cultures. Saltburn is a surfing town, famous for its historic pier and coastal cliff, and it's a Mecca for surfer dudes and skaters. My bedsit was in a big old concrete building that was used to house a lot of ex-cons. The whole place smelled of weed and it was an absolute dump. My room was tiny and very basic, although I didn't see it as looking like a prison cell, as some of the X Factor crew did when they later came to film me there, for my homecoming video. This was just my life and what I was used to. I didn't expect any more, and I was grateful for what I had.

Once I moved to Saltburn I saw less of Dawson and all my old mates because they couldn't just walk around the corner to see me like they did before. They started to get jobs too, mostly in call centres, which meant they did twelve-hour shifts and had no social life. The dole office made me apply for jobs from time to time and I had to do courses about 'getting back to work' after I'd been signing on for so long. I did a few stints in offices and call centres, but I hated every minute and never stuck at anything.

I started to feel very lonely in my bedsit. I'd look out of the window and see the surfer dudes and hipsters outside and feel like such an ugly misfit by comparison. I didn't recognise it at the time, but I was suffering from depression, and I probably had been in Lumley Road too.

I wasn't educated about depression at all. If somebody had asked me back then what I thought a depressed person was like, I would probably have described someone who looked miserable all the time and moped around. This view didn't help when it came to understanding my mum's behaviour, of course. When she told us she had borderline personality disorder I was so ignorant about it, and looking back I think that made me sceptical. I couldn't see how someone with crippling depression could also be the bubbly, vibrant character she sometimes was. I never really got that Mam's mood swings were out of her control, and that her life was governed by her mental illness. Instead all I saw was a volatile, unpredictable person, and I resented Mam for the way she was, because whatever her mood, she made me live on my nerves and feel fearful when I was around her.

I didn't understand my own state either. If I passed one of my neighbours around my building I'd always say hello or exchange a bit of banter. I wanted to look normal and fit in – that was how I'd been my whole life – and because I was getting by and could do that, it never occurred to me that I was suffering from depression.

The reality was I was displaying a lot of the signs and symptoms that I now recognise very well. I wasn't motivated to get up in the day and do anything, and I was very down on myself and my situation. By that I mean I couldn't see the point of life, and when I thought about the future I saw and felt nothing. The future was a black space.

I had a mirror above the sink in the bedsit, and when I caught a glimpse of myself I'd recoil.

*You look disgusting. No wonder nobody wants you. I wouldn't even want you! No wonder you are all alone.*

When I look back on photographs from my late teens and early twenties there are some decent ones, and in some I even look quite handsome and in good shape. I couldn't see that then, not at all. Nobody could have convinced me that I was anything but an ugly, disgusting-looking misfit.

I started smoking weed on my own a lot. It was so easy to get hold of where I was living, and everyone around me smoked it. Sometimes I'd watch pop videos on the TV when I was high, and it was only then that I occasionally managed to glimpse the future and imagine I might still have one.

*That is the life you're meant to have, James. That could be you. It'll happen one day.*

I heard that voice quite a lot, but it sounded like it was coming from a place so far away from me it didn't seem real.

*You're at the bottom of the pile. You've got no money. You can't even eat properly. You're living in the most insignificant place on the planet. What is there to even get up for?*

This second voice was so much louder. It boomed in my head and I listened, because it sounded so much more convincing than the other one. I started to stay in bed longer and longer. Sometimes I didn't get up until 5 p.m., and even then I'd have no energy.

For three months I did next to nothing and lived like a virtual recluse, just staying in bed, smoking weed and writing songs bemoaning my miserable fate. Sometimes I'd look out the window and I'd see a group of lads walk past. They were in a very cool band I'd seen perform in a working club one time, and they called themselves Heroes and Hand Grenades. The lads reminded me of the punky kids on the TV show *Skins* and their music had Blink and Fightstar vibes. I thought they were sick, and I started to daydream about how good it would be to join their band.

One day I had the window open when they walked past and I decided to shout down to them, on a whim.

'Howay lads! I love your band!'

They looked up and all started shouting back. 'James Arthur, you're sick, man!' I was taken aback that they recognised me. I knew I had a reputation in Redcar for my music and all the gigs I'd done there, but I didn't expect these lads to know me.

Trav, the frontman of the band, asked if they could come up to the bedsit.

'Yeah, man! Come on up!' I shouted back; this was the best thing that had happened in all my time in the bedsit.

I sparked up a few joints and we all hung out together. I told the boys I liked bands that had a screamer as well as a singer, and I started to wonder if I could blag my way into their group. Trav played guitar as well as being the frontman, Alex was on bass, Josh was on the keyboard and Karl was the drummer. They were great lads, clearly very artistic and creative, and I could see they were all individual thinkers. I felt instantly comfortable in their company, and I told the lads again and again how cool I thought their band was.

'Well, why don't you join the band?'

'Really? I thought you'd never ask!'

I was buzzing. This was so brilliant for me, and the lads were happy too. They told me they wanted to be as well known as I was locally, and beyond. Music really mattered to all of them, and they wanted to see how far they could go with it.

We changed the name of the band to Heroes Fall First after I joined, and we practised all the time in the basement of Trav's house. Trav and me both screamed and played the guitar and our music was intense, like thrash metal. I loved every minute of being with the lads. I had a reason to get out of bed, and when I was making music I felt alive and connected to the world. The lads didn't scrap or take the piss out of each other and everything that was said was positive and inspiring. Josh, on keys, was so random, and was the wackiest, most hilarious guy you could meet. The whole group was quality; I'd never felt so at home with a bunch of lads before.

The only drawback was we were so heavy and intense we struggled to get gigs. We didn't do covers because we were adamant we wanted to perform our own music, and that didn't help at all. The only place that booked us regularly was the Ruby Street Social Club in Saltburn, where we played just once a fortnight. We lived for every gig, but it wasn't enough.

The dole office was still on at me to get a proper job, and for once I made an effort because I'd decided to learn to drive and wanted to earn some money to buy a car. I beat twelve other candidates to a job writing professional CVs for Pertemps, and I stuck at it for a month – long enough to save £200 to buy a battered Rover 200. Then I stopped turning up and was dismissed.

I could not have cared less about being sacked. The band was going places. Trav left and was replaced by a guy called Matty, another great character, and I stepped up as the frontman. We agreed to tone things down and not scream any more, so we started to sound more like Taking Back Sunday, and we also changed our name, to Save Arcade. That's when things really started to take off.

We wrote seven songs and made an EP, *Superhero*, which included our biggest song, 'The Truth'. It became a hit on the pop-punk circuit and we started to build a fan base online and get booked for bigger and bigger gigs, even headlining some shows in the North-East.

*This is it! This is what you've always dreamed of. You're gonna make it!*

The buzz I felt on stage was incredible, and afterwards I always felt like I did as a boy in the school performance, feeling so wired that I couldn't sleep.

*I can't sleep, Mam, I just want to keep talking about it! What the hell was that? That buzz is like nothing else. How can we get some more of it, Mam?*

What I'd said in Bahrain ran through my head so many times, because at last I was getting that buzz again and again. I'd found the way to get some more of it, and this was what I wanted to do forever.

The boys in the band had become like a proper pack of brothers to me, and we were hanging out together 24/7. I loved it. My mood was so much better and the more successful we became the more exciting life was. We had all the parties and loads of fun; it was quality.

On the night before my driving test all the lads were drinking and Karl was so off his head he smashed a guitar on his forehead and split it open.

'We're all fucked but you need to go to hospital. Come on!'

I'd been smoking weed but I hadn't been drinking. The five of us squashed into my clapped-out Rover, despite the fact it had no insurance and I had no licence. It was a Friday night and I drove twenty-five minutes to the nearest hospital, where we had to wait two hours in A&E for Karl to get patched up. It was four in the morning by the time we were on our way back to the flat, and I got pulled over by the police and breathalysed. I was given the all-clear as I hadn't been drinking and the officer didn't notice I'd been smoking weed, but he said he'd have to take my car off me for having no insurance or licence.

'But I've saved so hard, officer, working at Pertemps to pay for my car,' I pleaded. 'My best friend was badly injured and nobody else was fit to drive. What choice did I have? I couldn't leave him to bleed to death, could I?'

I had the gift of the gab in those days: one of my party tricks was to make prank calls, pretending to be a Scottish radio DJ called Big Willy Mack. I loved playing a character and putting on an act, and I got so many people with those calls. It was hilarious and addictive. Anyhow, Karl looked suitably wretched, showing the officer the large bandage wrapped round his head. Unbelievably we got let off, and we drove away giggling like schoolboys. We even had the cheek to go to McDonald's on the way home – and the next day I passed my test.

Life was good, and not only did we have all the parties, but now the band was doing so well, we also had all the girls.

*Why is she interested in me? Can't she see what I can see?*

There were so many times when I got with a beautiful girl and honestly could not believe what was happening. It was like being in primary school all over again, and having Sophie, the prettiest girl in the class, wanting to be my girlfriend. It was thrilling and terrifying all at the same time. I was so paranoid and self-critical I always thought someone might be playing a trick on me, or I might wake up the next day and find out it had all been some crazy, trippy dream.

By now I was smoking as much weed as I could get hold of every single day and I was hardly eating, because I preferred to spend my money on weed. Occasionally one of the lads would turn up with a pizza and I'd think I was in paradise.

'No way, man! Weed *and* pizza! Life doesn't get any better than this.'

It did get better. In April 2010, we got our biggest gig ever, supporting Mayday Parade at the Middlesbrough Empire. We played to a crowd of more than 1,200 and I was completely blown away. The feeling it gave me, being on that stage, was like nothing on earth.

*This is it. This is what I am going to do for the rest of my life.*

I could see the future clearly now. All I'd ever dreamed of was coming true, and Mam had been right all along. This was my path in life; this was what I was born to do.

# CHAPTER TWENTY-TWO

*Don't listen to the demons, James. You're
in a better place now. You've got this.*

'James, I think it's time to stop apologising. It's time to move on.'

I was at Simon Cowell's house in London. He'd invited me, Neil and Russell over to talk about the possibility of Syco re-signing me. It was a whole year after our phone conversation, when I'd pleaded my case and told Simon I wanted to be the best thing to ever come out of *The X Factor*. In the meantime, I'd continued to write music and perform at gigs and events in Europe, and James Grant had continued to stand by me and do all they could to support me and get me a record deal for my next album.

I was so grateful to Neil and Martin and everyone at James Grant for sticking with me. When they started to manage my finances, it emerged I was £196,000 in debt, with £90,000 of that owed to my previous management. I'd had no idea things were that bad and we had crisis talks about whether I should declare myself bankrupt. I was twenty-four hours away from doing that when Mark, my new accountant, came up with a plan that meant I could cling on, just, as long as he and everybody else agreed they wouldn't get paid for a while. It was possible James Grant would never break even with me, but their attitude was that they'd committed to helping me and they trusted in my talent, so they were standing by me. I couldn't thank them enough. What I appreciated most of all was that they were all genuine people who were very straight with me. I'd been given a day-to-day manager, Helen Gilliat, who was also there from the start, championing me and supporting me non-stop. Helen is from Hull, and I liked hearing her friendly Yorkshire accent every day. I felt connected, and part of something again.

I kept working hard on my music and there was some good news eventually, when Sony Germany called to say they were interested in me, having seen how popular I was with fans in Europe. Martin, Helen and Russell flew out and played some songs to them and they really liked the tracks and signed me up, on their Columbia label. It was the lifeline I was praying for, and I was so grateful.

I started to get some good sessions and it was great that I could finish my album with Columbia, but I was still fretting about being re-signed with Syco. I had a lot of angst-ridden conversations with Jess about my future. Our relationship was strained by everything that had happened and we'd broken up several times, but whatever happened, Jess was always a good friend to me and was there to support me.

'What am I doing all this for? Simon dangled a carrot in that phone call but it's come to nothing. I might as well face it, I'm never going to get back the career I want.'

I knew full well that without being signed up by any other UK label, I wouldn't get played on Radio 1 and Capital. Without that exposure, I'd struggle to break through, and I would never get back on the X *Factor* stage and make the fairy-tale comeback I dreamed of. Jess always consoled me and tried to get me to stay positive, but there were lots of times when all I wanted to do was sit in a dark room on my own, watching TV, which I did a lot.

Me and Jess had managed to have a holiday to Thailand in the immediate aftermath of my self-destruction. I stood in the sea, sometimes for hours at a time, looking back at the palm trees on the beach and appreciating the paradise I was in. It was so healing. I felt connected to the planet, and a million miles away from my demons. When I felt angst-ridden about being re-signed by Syco I tried to meditate and take myself back to that peaceful place. Jess taught me how to do that, and she never stopped paying me compliments about my music, encouraging me to be positive and doing everything she could to help improve my mental health. Jess could not have done more, but when I was obsessing about what was going to happen with my career I doubted absolutely every-thing and lapsed into paranoia.

*What is Jess even doing here? What's her motive? I've got no money, no career. What does she want from me? She could have anyone, and look at me. Look at the state of me. I'll never get re-signed. I'm a loser and I've lost it all. There's no going back.*

When I was invited to the meeting at Simon's house I hoped it might finally be the turning point I longed for. When Neil, Russell and I arrived, it was like walking into judges' houses, because Simon lives in a huge, luxury mansion. The whole thing had me shook. It reminded me of being in Dubai, preparing to sing for Nicole and Ne-Yo when I was strung out on Prozac.

*This is all going to go to shit. Why are you even bothering?*

*Don't listen to the demons, James. You're in a better place now. You've got this. You can do it. You have to do it.*

Butlers offered us mini hamburgers – or sliders, as they called them – and Simon appeared, smiling in sunglasses. He said I looked good, which reminded me he was interested in my welfare as well as my music. Sonny, then the president of Syco, was with him and I'd taken two tracks to perform – 'The Truth' and 'Promise'.

I started off with an apology to the label, for all my mistakes of the past, and that's when Simon told me I had to stop apologising.

'Stop the apology songs, too. You've said it now. Have you got some songs there?'

I picked up my guitar and prepared to sing. I'd never performed in front of Simon or Sonny before and I felt self-conscious. I had flashbacks of performing at home for Mam, or for Dawson. I wished I had glass French doors to hide behind, or that I could turn off the lights, but I couldn't.

Before I got started Simon started chatting to me about what type of women I like; I think he was probably just trying to settle me down.

'Do you like crazy girls?' he asked. 'I always seem to get involved with crazy girls!'

I laughed. 'Yes, I'm the same,' I said. 'The crazier the better.'

It was just banter, but it worked. I felt a rapport there, and I realised I didn't see Simon as a scary music mogul. I never had, in fact. To me he's a chancer, a hustler; a nice guy who's done really well for himself. He cares about other people and that's why he's good at finding out what the public like. I respected him and I wanted to do my very best.

When I finished performing my songs I told Simon I could write him a thousand more. 'I've got hit upon hit, any genre you like,' I said.

Maybe I sounded more like a double-glazing salesman than a credible artist, but Simon grinned.

'I like that attitude, James. I don't know what it is about you. You're a bit odd, but most super-talented people are. That's what makes you what you are.' There was a pause, and he swapped a look with Sonny. 'We're really interested in you.'

We came away thinking it had been a great meeting and that I was in with a good chance of going back to Syco, but then it all went very quiet and nothing transpired, month after month. I carried on doing sessions and working on my album, and James Grant began approaching other labels. They also put in several thousand pounds to help me get the album marketed in the UK, as without being signed to a British label we had no distribution network and none of the publicity that entailed.

Meanwhile I went to LA to do some sessions. Columbia had given me a fantastic A&R, a lady called Ina Jedlicka. She loved my tracks but she said we didn't have a single from my album yet, and that was what she was focusing on now.

My mate Jamie came out to stay with me in LA and one day we sat in an Irish bar, drinking whiskey and putting the world to rights like lads do. Man United were playing Liverpool and we watched the game and stayed in the bar until 2 a.m. the next day. I was hung over when I woke up later that morning. I knew I had a session with a big producer and so I'd texted Ina the day before and asked exactly what she wanted. It's not my style to write to a brief at all, but I didn't want to waste anyone's time. Fortunately, as it happened, Ina had a very clear idea in her head.

'I'd like the storytelling of Lukas Graham's "7 Years" and the easy listening vibe of Justin Beiber's "Love Yourself".'

'OK. You should have just said!' I joked. 'I could do that in my sleep.'

I went down to the session and 'Say You Won't Let Go' wrote itself in two hours, with minimal help. I just started singing a melody I had in my head and the lyrics began to pour out of me. It was simple. I was telling the story of meeting a girl and falling in love, and what it would be like to spend the rest of your life with her. I had this thought that it's so hard to keep hold of love in this day and age. There are so many distractions, and the words 'say you won't let go' seemed to sum up what I wanted to say. It was a powerful plea from the heart, about what I think most of us wish for.

I played the track to Jamie, and Jess heard it too. I said I thought it was a beautiful love song and would maybe make track five on the album, but not the first single, as it wasn't a representation of the album. Jamie and Jess both loved it, and then Ina completely lost her mind over it.

'This is it!' she said. 'This is the single! I love it. This has to be it.'

I really wasn't sure. I was very uncomfortable that the track I'd spent the least amount of time over would be the first single from my album and I argued against it, quite ferociously. I thought we needed a redemption song, rather than a love song, and I got angry when Ina dug her heels in.

'Are you seriously saying that I've been through hell and have been pouring my heart out writing music for this album for two years, and the first song people are gonna hear me release is this – a song you gave me a brief for and was written in a couple of hours? No way!'

The label and management all agreed with Ina and suddenly everyone involved in the album started telling me, 'This is the song that's gonna get you back to where you want to be.' Nobody was saying it was going to go to number one or be a global hit, but everybody at Columbia and James Grant agreed it had every chance of being the hit I needed to get me back on the map. In the end, I relented and listened to them all; they are very talented people, after all. Ina especially had never stopped fighting for the song, and now she was very excited, which started to rub off on me. I began to feel optimistic, and I started to dare to hope good things would happen.

The single was set for release in September 2016, which was just a few months away, but we still had no UK deal. We'd tried all the labels at Sony, and one by one they'd all passed on signing me up. Then every other record label we approached followed suit, and we got a depressing string of rejections, one after the other. Syco was the only label that hadn't got back to us yet and I still held out hope, even as the release date edged closer and closer.

I went on a night out with my old friends in Redcar towards the end of August, about three weeks before the single was due to drop. I'd got myself in really good shape and was down to thirteen and a half stone, my optimum weight. I felt good, and I was determined to be upbeat about my comeback, with or without Syco. I'd discussed a strategy with James Grant and we had a publicity campaign in place. We talked about me giving some interviews to the press and TV to made it very clear how sorry I was for past mistakes, and to discuss my mental health problems. I wanted people to understand what I'd been through, and to focus on my music instead of my past behaviour.

'Shall we go out before the fight or after?' I asked the lads.

'Let's go out first and come back for the fight.'

It was a fateful decision. It was the night of the Conor McGregor v Nate Diaz rematch and I was really looking forward to it. I'm a huge fan of UFC and have followed the sport for a long time, not for the human cock-fighting element, but because I like to see a chess match in the ring. I love mixed matches, seeing a wrestler going up against a boxer, and I became a massive fan of Conor after discovering him in 2014, at exactly the time I lost my record deal. I heard him talking about visualisation and the power of attraction and, because of my situation, I was fascinated. 'Within two years I'll be world champion of UFC,' he declared. His self-belief was unshakable. 'I'll take over the entire featherweight division, and then I'll get the lightweight belt. You mark my words.'

I did mark his words, and I tried to grab hold of some of his self-assurance and optimism. It was because of Conor that I started to visualise myself back on the X *Factor* stage, having made my triumphant comeback. I watched all Conor's videos and became obsessed by him. To my mind, he's the best trash talker in the business; an Irish Muhammad Ali. I watched in awe as he won fight after fight and even predicted the rounds. I was so inspired by him, and I was really looking forward to seeing him prove his latest prediction.

Before the fight, me and the lads decided to go to the Plimsoll Line pub in Redcar, one of my old haunts. We had a drink and then a couple of the lads wanted a cigarette so we went outside. When we came back in we'd lost our seats so we started walking through the pub looking for somewhere else to sit. We hadn't even finished our first drink at this point.

BANG. I felt something hit the back of my head and it felt strange. Danny was behind me and for a moment I wondered why he'd slapped me on the back of the head so hard. BANG. Then came a second blow and it rocked me to the core. It felt like a really hard punch. I stumbled forward and as I turned around I saw one of my other mates drag a guy down behind me. I realised then that this man had attacked me, but I had no idea why or who he was, and I was so confused. I put my hand to the back of my head and it was covered in blood.

It turned out I'd been hit with a glass the first time, then hit very hard with a fist. My mates got me out of the pub and took me round to my dad's house, as it's very close by. They called an ambulance and I was taken to hospital in shock. I had a seven-centimetre gash and a very bad headache, and I needed six staples to hold the wound together. I couldn't believe it, and when I got over the initial shock I started panicking about my comeback in a major way.

*What if this single comes off and does well? What if I do end up being invited back on the* X Factor *stage? This is so depressing. I might not be able to deal with this now my head's split open.*

I couldn't get over my bad luck. I wanted to enjoy the run-up to the single and I wanted to come back and make a good impression with my image as well as my music. I'd taken so much stick in the past for my appearance, and I wanted people to say 'James Arthur's back and look how well he's looking.' I'd done my best in the intervening years. I'd straightened my teeth and had my eyes lasered, and I'd worked hard to get my weight down. I was ready, but after the attack I had to lie on a couch for three weeks as my head healed. I was worried I'd gain weight, and I felt sorry for myself.

My mood plummeted as I lay there recuperating, day after day. Even Conor McGregor's victory failed to lift me out of my depression.

*Conor can triumph and live up to his promises and dreams, but you can't, James. This isn't your journey. You weren't supposed to do this. This is your karma, your just deserts for all your wrongdoings of the past.*

I'd gone vegetarian a few months earlier, which had helped me get my weight down. I managed to stick to my veggie diet, but I started comfort eating, having loads of bread and toast and stodgy crap. My weight began to creep up and I also started to freak myself out by reading about head injuries. I read that a head trauma can affect your eyesight and make you have slurred speech. People have died in the aftermath of a blow to the head.

*Oh my God. You have spent two years working on this album and it's now two weeks to go before the first single drops. You're gonna die, James, before the record is released. 'Say You Won't Let Go'? YOU are going, James. LET GO! This is the end.*

'I need an ambulance please, right away.'

I was gasping for breath and my heart had gone into overdrive. I started having daily panic attacks that were so severe I was back and forth to the hospital, having my heart checked as well as my head. The only thing that rescued me – besides being reassured by a paramedic or a doctor that I wasn't having a heart attack – was forcing myself to visualise my future success, just like Conor McGregor. The vision was buried deep now, but it was still there in the back of my mind. I'd try very hard to picture myself on the X *Factor* stage again, and I'd flick to that image as often as I could, just to stay alive.

In my most lucid moments, I did not honestly believe my comeback would work. I put on a brave face with family and friends, saying to them, 'When I've made my comeback . . .' but really I only said it because I thought I stood a better chance of it coming true if I put it out there, to the universe. In reality I felt it was too big a dream, and it couldn't possibly come true. The blow to the head had been my reality check; it was a warning bell that life was not going to work out as I wanted it to, and I had to wake up, face facts and get real.

It was now only a week to go to the single release, and we still hadn't heard back either way from Syco, which did nothing to help my feelings of gloom and paranoia. Then we finally got an email with their response, and it couldn't have been worse news.

'We're going to pass I'm afraid.'

*Fuck. Fuck. Fuck.*

When the news was relayed to me I felt completely broken.

This had all been a massive waste of time and I was absolutely devastated.

'What am I doing this for?' I complained to Russell. I felt so desperate. 'This can't be it. Why? I just can't do this any more. It's all a complete and utter waste of time without a UK label supporting me.'

I ranted to Russell on the phone at length, several times, and in the end, I could barely breathe. Everyone at James Grant tried to console me. They told me we'd come this far and should carry on and do our best, putting the single out online and pushing on with our own publicity and marketing. I had a lot of loyal fans – the JArmy, as they are known – and we would have to rely on them to pick it up. I did have faith in the fans, as they'd stayed incredibly supportive of me for so long, and I had to admit we had nothing to lose. We had a video ready to go and Russell had lined up two major interviews – one with the *Sun*, and one on *This Morning*.

'OK, let's just do it,' I said. There was really no other option. We would drop the single as a digital download only, on Friday, 9 September.

The day before, I gave a Facebook live interview to Dan Wootton at the *Sun* – my first in two and a half years. I was a nervous wreck beforehand. I didn't sleep and I was overthinking everything. I looked a mess when I turned up, with my hair half in curtains and half swept to one side. Neil from James Grant tried to calm me down. He'd given me loads of pep talks over the previous few months, often taking me out for a coffee so we could relax and just chat. 'You can do this,' he said. 'You can inspire people. Be yourself and be honest, and one day we'll be sitting at the Brit Awards and you'll be writing a book about this!'

In the event Dan Wootton helped a lot too. He was supportive and asked all the right questions, and I felt able to simply tell the truth, about my mental health and how fame nearly destroyed me. I was very grateful to Dan for how he steered me through the interview, but nevertheless I felt sick when I waited for the public's reaction. I had no idea how people would respond to me or to my new music, and I was shaking with nerves.

*If none of this works out you might as well be dead, James. There's nothing left for you.*

I had no fight left to argue. There was nothing more I could do. I was exhausted and very scared, because I had no control over what was going to happen next.

# CHAPTER TWENTY-THREE

*Be more confident. Show your eyes! Be who you are, James*

After our biggest ever gig at the Middlesbrough Empire, Save Arcade started to get a few people interested who promised to take us to the next level. We felt on the crest of a wave and I was more optimistic than I'd ever been. Life was good, and I even got a better flat, on Emerald Street in Saltburn. The lads practically lived with me, especially Karl, and we started to party even harder than before.

I'd built a few bridges with Mam, and she was in a good

place too. She'd moved to a new house in nearby Marske and was single again, and she was also in party mode. Just like she'd done in the past when her mood was up, Mam became the ultimate fun-time Frankie; the hostess with the mostest. I'd go over to see her when she had the house full of her mates and I'd always have a really good time. Mam was at her vivacious best, telling anyone who'd listen how talented and amazing I was, and it was so uplifting to be around her.

One of her friends was ten years younger than Mam and ten years older than me, and I'd never come across someone so sexually flirtatious in my life before. I was fascinated by her and I ended up sleeping with her. It was wild. It was like the life I left behind when Mam threw me out had happened in some parallel universe. I wasn't a worthless, aggravating boy any more, and I wasn't the black sheep of the family. It was surreal, and I lapped it up.

Mam had started doing some life coaching and would talk to me about thinking positively. She has a way with words that strikes you in the heart, and when she was in this frame of mind her encouragement was phenomenal; it filled me to the brim with optimism. Whatever had gone on between us, Mam's belief in my voice had never waned, and the combination of having her incredibly enthusiastic support and enjoying success with Save Arcade was intoxicating. I was addicted to the buzz I got at a gig and I wanted more and more. I never wanted that adrenaline supply to run out, not ever.

I was stoned every single time I did a gig, and I'd started experimenting with harder drugs. I took MDMA and M-CAT (i.e. Ecstasy and mephedrone). They were readily available and I didn't worry about the consequences. I just saw them as innocent party drugs – types of amphetamines, a bit like speed. The drugs made me feel outside reality, which was where I liked to be. Stupidly, I started to spend weeks on end on those drugs, to the point where they *became* my reality and I came to depend on them. I didn't see it happening. I felt invincible. I was convinced Save Arcade was going to get signed by a record label any time soon, and then my whole future would be mapped out.

It didn't happen like that. One by one all the promises we were made after the Middlesbrough Empire gig gradually came to nothing. I was devastated.

'Was that it? Was that the pinnacle of our career? No way, man! It can't be!'

I couldn't accept it, and for a long time I tried to cling on to the hope that something would give, a recording deal would somehow transpire and Save Arcade would finally make it outside the North-East. The lads wanted to believe it would happen too, but the fact was we didn't have the money we needed to take things further ourselves and it was time to face reality and make choices. The other lads were all starting to get pressure from their parents to get proper jobs. Alex signed up for a plumbing course and Karl was talking about going to college. I had nobody telling me what to do and I didn't want to give up the band and get a job, even though I was so skint I was falling behind with the rent on my Emerald Street flat and eventually had to ask my landlord to let me have the old bedsit back.

'Come on, lads, let's keep going until we're thirty and see what happens,' I said. I meant it, but the other lads were growing up and moving on. I felt left behind. Save Arcade was falling apart, and then something happened that finished the band off completely.

I had Jazz staying with me for a bit, because things weren't good between her and Mam and she was going off the rails. I worried about taking my little sister in, because of the drugs and the lifestyle I was leading. My set-up was far from ideal, but I figured it was better for her to stay with me than to get kicked out on the streets and sleep rough like I did.

Jazz was still only sixteen and was in a vulnerable place in every sense. She had stayed with me before, when I first moved into my bedsit. Jazz had my bed and I slept on the sofa, and we were so skint we lived on nothing but noodles. I'd always felt super-protective of Jazz, and when she stayed with me these feelings deepened. I looked on her more as a daughter than my little sister, and I truly became a father figure to her. Our relationship has stayed like that ever since, and I will never stop looking out for Jazz and protecting her as much as I can.

So then when I got the impression that one of lads around the band might have something on with a girl who'd come over to visit us, whether I was right about that or not, it ruined everything for me. Worried about my little sister in a household of lads coming and going, in an instant I completely lost my mind.

It felt like my whole world had been blown apart. I'd known these lads for three years and we were incredibly tight-knit. They knew I had trust issues and was paranoid about being stabbed in the back. That was it. They were not my brothers any more. We were done, completely. I didn't want them in my life, and there was only one way forward for me: I was going to make it on my own, as a solo artist.

After Save Arcade I suffered withdrawal symptoms, both from the band and the drugs.

*Avoid the spaces in between. Stay on the pavement. Don't fall through the cracks.*

I had a warning voice in my head, but I ignored it. I was super-stubborn about the boys and refused to have anything whatsoever to do with them. I started shutting myself away, spending hours on my own, smoking weed non-stop and writing songs about betrayal.

My paranoia was heightened by the drugs I took. I'd started to notice that when I came down from them I had mood swings and would kick off about nothing. I decided I wanted to come off MDMA and M-CAT completely, but when I tried it was horrendous and I really struggled.

Facing the day scared the life out of me. I couldn't function normally; my paranoia was off the scale and the only time I felt relatively sane was when I was baked on weed.

*What are you looking at? Are you laughing at me? Do I look ugly?*

I'd even think like that when I was alone in the room watching TV and a face was looking back at me from the screen. My answer was to smoke another joint, to try to shut out the scary world I was facing. I thought I was going crazy, and I didn't want to live that way.

Eventually, life was so unbearable I admitted to myself I needed help. I knew I couldn't get through this on my own and felt so desperate I went to the GP. He diagnosed severe depression, and that's when I was prescribed the antidepressant Sertraline for the first time. It helped me finally kick the party drugs, and in the short term it did have a positive effect on my mood.

*What are you doing this for? This is not you. Be more confident. Show your eyes! Be who you are, James.*

I was staring in the mirror, looking at my hair pulled over my right eye, as it had been for years. I pushed it back so I could see my full face. Then I examined my eye, trying to detect the turn I always thought was so visible.

*What are you looking at, weirdo?*

I couldn't see the turn in my eye, and I wondered if other people didn't see it either. It was the first time I'd ever considered that perhaps I wasn't bong-eyed after all.

*There's nothing there! What are you talking about?*

I'd been going out with my girlfriend Lucy for several months by this time. We met in a local church hall, where Mam's friend was organising a talent show and had asked me to help out. Lucy sang and then she asked if she could do a duet with me.

'I might get in here,' I thought, because that was my mentality then. I'd had two serious relationships since leaving home, one with another girl called Lucy and one with Emma. During the time I dated Emma her dad had Motor Neurone Disease. I was in love with Emma, and watching her family pull together as he deteriorated was inspiring and made me want to appreciate my family more.

Luckily for me, when I met Lucy at the talent show she was really into the skinny, scruffy, worn-out rock-and-roll look. She was impressed I was in a band, as I was still with Save Arcade then, and we hit it off. I liked Lucy a lot, but I was scared of messing up her life. She came from such a decent, well-to-do family, and I wasn't emotionally available because of all my issues, which made me feel guilty that I might be a burden to her.

The first time Lucy took me home to meet her parents I felt mortified for being a scruffy stoner who was on the dole. Her mum and dad were incredibly kind and patient, and they always tried to help me out. I even lived with them for a while, because there was a gap between me leaving Emerald Street and getting my bedsit back. Lucy's parents did so much to support me, but when I was in their house I always had voices in my head telling me I was worthless, and I was a misfit. Ultimately, however welcome Lucy's mum and dad tried to make me feel, I always knew I was nowhere near good enough for their daughter, and I never felt at ease staying with them.

*You're scum, James. You don't belong. What are you even doing? This is all messed up. You're a loser and a misfit. This will end in tears. How can you do this?*

I lived in permanent fear I would end up disappointing or hurting Lucy, and I found it so hard to conform to any kind of conventional lifestyle after being such a drifter for so long. As soon as I got my bedsit back I couldn't wait to escape there.

I'd often borrow £10 from Lucy to buy a 'tenner bit' of weed – enough to get very stoned. I'd lock my door and smoke the lot, and I'd also pop my antidepressant pills at the same time, taking one or two, depending how low I felt. The combination had replaced my addiction to M-CAT and MDMA. The Sertraline curbed my depression, and the weed gave me the lift I needed so I didn't feel numb and emotionless. I was convinced I'd hit on a winning formula.

The more Sertraline and weed I took, the more I began to shut everybody out of my life. I didn't want to be around people, and the initial lift I'd had from the antidepressants was gone. I went back to having no reason to get up in the morning and I'd spend days in bed, and days on end on my own. When Lucy came over she'd get dragged into my lifestyle and would stay in bed with me until 5 p.m. I asked her all the time what she was doing with a loser like me. She said she loved me, but I was totally confused, because I had absolutely nothing going for me and was living such a sad and miserable existence.

I'd watch *American Idol* on TV when I was high and on my own at night, and I'd have some wild fantasies about going on the show and winning it. I remembered my friends telling me I should go on *Pop Idol*, and me being so dismissive of them, because I believed one hundred per cent I was going to make it on my own. My confidence in my talent was still super-strong, but I was starting to lose faith that my break was just going to materialise, as if my magic. I was nearly twenty-three, and I've always been obsessive and superstitious about that number. I had it in my head that if I didn't make it by that age I was finished, and the thought was terrifying, and began playing on my mind all the time.

Even though I was in such a dark place I was still managing to do gigs on my own again, performing cover sets in the Vic, another local pub. They paid for my rent and my weed; my essentials. Eventually a guy called John McGough noticed me there and started showing interest in me. He played the saxophone in the same pub for another singer, Caterina Rea – a relative of Chris Rea – and he had some impressive connections in the industry, one of them being the dance DJ and record producer Carl Cox, who'd worked at Ibiza's legendary Café del Mar. John had also played on some big gigs, including an *X Factor* tour, and I was impressed by him.

'I could get you heard by some pretty big people,' John told me. 'If you could get some demos together this could take off. I've got some songs and I could record you.'

'Woah! Really?'

*What were you worried about? This is finally it! This is gonna be your ticket, at long last. It was always gonna happen after all!*

I thought that John McGough was the guy I'd been waiting for all these years, and that I could finally make something of this bullshit, impoverished lifestyle I was living. I recorded a couple of his songs and John really took me under his wing. He talked to me about cleaning up my lifestyle and eating better and he even took me to the gym, because he could see I was malnourished and skinny and needed some help in that respect.

I was still relying on my daily doses of Sertraline and weed to get through the day, but one night I messed with my usual formula, and I popped three Sertraline pills. I don't remember why, because one or two had always been my limit. I guess I thought this dose would simply give me a bigger lift from my low mood than normal, but it didn't. I was watching *American Idol* again, stoned, and as I took the pills I was laughing to myself, thinking, 'What if I did this show? Maybe I should?' I loved watching Jennifer Lopez and Randy Jackson and I thought they did it so well. They had a live band and the whole set-up was just so sick. Imagine going on and winning a show like that?

Suddenly I started fighting for breath. My heart was pumping crazily, my brain was throbbing and the TV screen was out of focus. I thought I was having a seizure or an epileptic fit, and it was terrifying.

*You've wrecked your brain, James. You've messed up your wiring. Fuck! You've done it this time. What the hell have you done? You need help. You need help fast.*

I felt so vulnerable. I could have been two years old again, having just crashed face first into the glass coffee table. I needed help, and I needed someone to take care of me, because I couldn't look after myself.

*Nobody understands me better than Mam. I need my mum.*

I went to Mam's, and when I knocked on her door I was thinking I was going to either end up completely brain damaged or dead.

Mam was absolutely brilliant. She asked me exactly what I had taken and then talked to me very gently and calmly, the way I'd seen her speak to some of the people she did life coaching for.

'Listen to me, darlin'. You need to come off everything. The weed, the antidepressants. They're not helping you. You have this opportunity with John McGough and you need to be in the best possible state to make the most of it. I'll help you.'

I listened, I cut out everything, there and then, and I agreed to stay with Mam and do a detox. It was the first time in years I wasn't on anything at all, and when the withdrawal symptoms kicked in I felt absolutely wretched. My nerves were on edge and I felt so paranoid and uneasy in my skin, but I knew I had to do this. I felt very strongly that if I didn't, I'd kill my brain and my life would be over.

Mam knew a lot about the power of positive therapy, and she got me to watch videos of the American life coach Tony Robbins. I wasn't sure about him at first. It sounded like happy-clappy mumbo jumbo, but Mam didn't give up. She told me to give him a chance, because Tony Robbins had inspired so many people. I listened, but when I tried to focus on Mam's computer screen to watch the videos I suddenly freaked out. I was convinced I had the devil inside me, and that was so frightening. I was convinced I'd done long-term psychological damage, and I was willing to try anything to claw back some kind of sanity.

Listening to Tony Robbins did motivate me, and then Mam suggested I did 'primal screaming' to rid myself of the terrible feeling I had the devil inside me, and to free myself of all the other demons I had lurking in my heart and mind. I'd never really understood what primal screaming was before, and I'd normally have been so sceptical of something like that, but I was in such a dark place I was willing to try anything.

'I'll do whatever it takes,' I told Mam. 'I have to sort myself out. I can't carry on like this. Tell me what to do.'

'Just scream to your heart's content, into the pillow,' Mam said. 'Let it all out. You'll be surprised how good it feels.'

I lay on her couch and screamed blue murder into a pillow, for hours and hours. I had flashbacks to being a boy, crying deliriously into my pillow in my bunk bed in Winchester Road. All the pain and trauma I'd been through in the past sped through my head, like a video on fast forward.

Mam also played me videos from the spoken-word poetry show *Def Poetry Jam*, which blew my mind, but in a very good way. It reminded me of how my lyrics could inspire other people, just like the poets' words got through to me. I thought back to when I sang to Mam through the French doors when I was a teenager, and how she was so moved and complimentary about my music. I realised I'd forgotten the lesson I'd learned that day, about how I could gain so much satisfaction from connecting with other people through my songs. I'd spent too long stuck in a rut, thinking my songs were all about me again, and doing nothing but complain about how messed up I was in my lyrics. Now, thanks to Mam, I felt motivated to be more positive again, and to make music that mattered, and could get through to other people.

I wrote about twenty songs in the space of a week because my brain was super-active, and the process helped me cope with the anxiety brought on by my withdrawal, because it distracted me from dwelling on how fractious and jittery I felt.

Unfortunately, me and Mam had a big row after I'd been staying with her for twelve days. It had been good while it lasted, but the argument flicked an instant switch in my brain. We rowed about my time in foster care, I think. Mam was always in denial, and when I brought it up as we chatted about my issues, she tried to tell me I'd only been in care for a few weeks, rather than two and a half years or so, which it had been in reality. She flipped out when I argued back, and then it was game over.

I bounced, walking the two and a half miles from Mam's house back to my bedsit. Then, after my twelve-day detox, I popped a pill and rolled myself a joint. I needed both drugs, that's what I told myself. My addictive brain won. I had to have the combination of pills and weed, because nothing else could help me feel better at that moment in time, and I didn't care about tomorrow. I put my feet up and sat there in absolute bliss. In that moment, the feeling was something else.

I told John McGough I wanted to play in a band again, as well as recording songs. He supported me and we sourced a blues guitarist, Jez, and a guy called Chris for keys. An old mate of mine called Rich Doney was on bass. Rich had helped me a lot over the years with recording tracks for MySpace, and it was great to have him on board. Finally, we got Jordan Swain from my old band Moonlight Drive to play drums, which was a massive coup as he was so talented. We called ourselves The James Arthur Band and did a few gigs, but most of all we recorded songs and made some EPs together, and we put them online under the name The James Arthur Project.

Our music went down very well with fans and local audiences, but ultimately nothing happened in terms of getting picked up by a label and getting a record deal. The eventual realisation that this had been yet another dead end knocked me deep into depression, and for the first time ever I thought I might as well give up on my dream.

*I told you to avoid the spaces in between. You've fallen through the cracks, James. You're down too deep. You're never gonna get up from this.*

I had no fight left in me to answer the demons back and I spent months wallowing in my depression, fearing the future and wondering if I even had one. Mam and Lucy both had my back, and they refused to give up on me, or let me give up on myself.

'James, *The X Factor* has a mobile van in town,' Mam said. 'You have to get yourself down there. This is your chance.'

Mam texted me over and over again, and when I eventually took her £10 for my train fare to Middlesbrough, it was touch and go whether I would blow the cash on a tenner bit of weed instead of going to the audition.

To this day, I'm not sure how I managed to make the right choice, because I felt so broken and beat. All I really wanted to do was curl up in a ball and forget about life, and if *The X Factor* had judged me on my mental health that day I would never have been allowed to audition.

I was a breakdown waiting to happen, a meltdown in the making. Nobody realised it, not even me.

# CHAPTER TWENTY-FOUR

*Enjoy this, James. This is special.*
*You need to savour this*

I was just about to get on a plane for a gig in Europe when my phone rang. It was the morning after we'd put 'Say You Won't Let Go' online and I was super-anxious. When I checked through airport security I started to panic, imagining this routine would become my whole life. If the single didn't make it, this was what I would have to carry on doing for the rest of my career.

*You're an exile, a deportee, an outcast. You can't work in the UK. Nobody wants you. You banished yourself. It's all your own fault. You might as well be dead.*

*Get a grip, James. Breathe. Keep breathing.*

'James, it's Russell.'

'Hi mate.'

I wasn't expecting any good news. Even though I had such loyal fans in the JArmy, and about two million followers on Twitter, I had to be realistic. I'd been away for two years and my music was different now. We had absolutely no idea how anybody was going to react to my song and I was too nervous and paranoid to get my hopes up.

'Something's happening, James.'

'What d'you mean?'

I could hear the excitement in Russell's voice.

'You're already in the top twenty on iTunes.'

'Are you jokin' me?'

'No, James. No joke.'

I couldn't believe it and I didn't know how to react. It's never been my style to spontaneously punch the air or jump up and down with excitement. That's a legacy from my childhood, when I'd wait to see what the mood was in the house to gauge how I was going to feel that day.

'Wow,' I said calmly. 'That's wild.'

In the back of my mind I'd always hoped I'd at least make the top sixty, so this was incredible.

Russell kept checking iTunes while I was on my flight, refreshing the download chart again and again. By the time I'd landed it was late morning and the song had climbed to number twelve.

It was such fantastic news, and one of those pivotal moments when I felt the ground shift beneath my feet. I was at another crossroads and the foundations of my life were moving, but in a good way this time. I was breathing normally. This was good news. This was absolutely amazing news, and now I was starting to digest it, react to it and believe it.

*Enjoy this, James. This is special. You need to savour this.*

During my recovery, I'd worked hard at teaching myself how to stand above my thoughts, to be aware of them, and watchful of them. I trained myself to do that because I needed to control my addictions. I needed to be able to step outside myself, look down on my behaviour and see when it was time to walk away from the table, go home, or switch the phone off.

The technique helped me in another way too, an unexpected way. I began to enjoy the positive benefits of being in the moment, of knowing when to take a look around and appreciate what was happening in the here and now. I never had that awareness when I was on *The X Factor*, or after I won it, but I did now. This was incredible news, and I knew I needed to enjoy it and appreciate it, right now.

So many good things started happening it was unreal. When I got home I had a meeting with the mental health charity Sane about becoming one of their ambassadors. My honesty about my mental health in the interview I did with the *Sun* had been very well received and I talked to Sane about how I could help promote their campaigns and encourage young people to talk about their mental health. It was so heartening to be in this position, and I felt very appreciative of everything that was going on.

Every day my single was climbing up the iTunes chart, and after just five days it went to number two. Russell called me.

We'd both been watching the download chart like excited hawks, and now we were buzzing and going crazy.

'Oh my god, James, it's insane!'

'I know, I'm in shock, man. Is this real?'

I was running out of words because there was good news after good news.

The next time Russell called he really took my breath away.

'James. I've just had a call from my boss. Syco want you back.'

'Syco want me back?'

'Yes. They've apologised and said they've made a huge mistake, and please can they re-sign you?'

'Syco want me back? What the fuck?'

'They want you to perform the single on this series of *The X Factor* too.'

It was heart-stopping, it really was. This was truly the stuff of movies and fairy tales.

'Neil was right, I need to write a book! You couldn't make this up. How many people get two chances like this?'

Syco had never re-signed an artist before and I loved the whole idea of making history in this way, although I have to admit there was a rebel demon in me that wanted to turn them down.

*Syco did nothing to help. You did this without them. Sony Germany and Columbia did this, and Russell and James Grant did this. Syco deserves no credit. Why should they come in now, when all the work is done?*

The old me would have been sucked into those negative thought patterns. There was certainly truth in them, but I knew better now. I wasn't going to sabotage an offer like this. I was done with self-destructing. I'm also a sucker for the underdog story, and I wanted this dream ending more than anything else in the world.

I thought back to the moment I won *The X Factor*, when I stood on the stage and somehow knew that wasn't it. Everything felt very different now. This *was* it. Finally, this was it. I sensed that very strongly. I'd done it my way, and it had worked.

I went on *This Morning* on the Friday, exactly a week after the single came out. I was so nervous about the interview I was pounding the treadmill in my flat every night leading up to it, to try to keep myself calm. On the way to the ITV studios I was trying very hard to breathe properly. All I could think was that I had to avoid having a panic attack on the sofa, in front of millions of TV viewers.

I knew what I wanted to say. I wanted to get across how embarrassed I was about all the mistakes I'd made in the past, and I didn't want to make any excuses. Eamonn Holmes and Ruth Langsford had my back, and when we got started they really helped me get my messages across. I discussed my mental health issues and explained how I hoped that making honest music would connect me to people again. I felt I'd done a good job of truthfully summing up what had happened to me over the previous few years, and the response from the public was positive, straight away. People were saying 'fair play' and 'good luck' all over social media, which really boosted me.

Later that same day the single went to number one on iTunes. I was sitting in my car, in London traffic, when I heard the news.

'Get in!' I started banging the steering wheel. 'Get in!'

The single was so far ahead on iTunes we knew it would be number one on the official chart the following week.

*You're going to be number one again, James. And you've done it all yourself this time. This is mental. This is insane!*

It felt very different to when 'Impossible' was climbing up the charts four years earlier. I wrote my song this time, and I felt one hundred per cent connected to it. This was phenomenal; I was buzzing so much.

I agreed to re-sign with Syco as my UK label, meaning my label right holders were now Syco, James Grant and Sony Germany. I owe a huge debt to all three parties, and Sony Columbia in the US. My total record deal was worth £1 million.

Russell was as giddy and knocked out as I was. 'Mate, can you believe we were on the verge of declaring you bankrupt less than a year ago? And now you've made yourself into a millionaire!'

I actually couldn't believe it, and I started to experience major fear. I felt like I was in a dream, a conscious dream, and I began to worry that something bad would happen and the dream would end. I racked my brains to try to remember if I'd done anything wrong in the past two years that might come to light and sabotage my comeback.

*You must have done something. This dream can't last. There is a girl out there. There's a photo out there. Something is going to come and get you, just like last time. What have you done, James?*

Every day I experienced paranoia and panic, imagining phantom horrors that were going to surface.

*What is it? When is it going to come out? You must have done something, James. Something or someone is going to ruin you all over again.*

*No, it won't happen. The photos don't exist. I've done*

*nothing wrong. There's no need to be anxious. Relax. Try to
enjoy this time. Enjoy your success, you've earned it.*

When my song became number one on the official chart I
finally went out and celebrated, with all the boys back home.
I had a lot of beer and watched a fight on TV, and then we
went out for food. Someone got me a 'Parmo', a famous
Middlesbrough dish. It's chicken cooked in breadcrumbs,
filled with a Parmesan sauce and topped with cheese. I was so
drunk I just tore into it, forgetting all about the fact I'd been
vegetarian for four months. I paid the price the next day,
because I went into my usual state of feeling guilty and super-
anxious about not being in control, and wondering what
other mistakes I might have made when I was intoxicated.

*You're number one, James. You're allowed a blow-out. Just
chill. Stop beating yourself up.*

The voice of reason was talking to me more and more, and
I listened to it and appreciated it. My negative thoughts and
anxious feelings were still there, but I was managing them
better and keeping things in perspective more. I was going for
days without coming close to a panic attack, and that was a
major breakthrough for me.

Now everything was geared towards getting my album out
and making sure it was as successful as the single. We brought
the release date forward to the end of October because the
single had done so well; it stayed at number one for three
weeks. I was listening to all the tracks from *Back from the
Edge* all the time, trying to mentally prepare myself for when
the album was released. Every song is so personal. I'd put my
heart and soul into each one, and I'd never worked so hard on
anything in my life before. I co-produced a lot of the tracks,
and I was super-fussy in the studio. I'd sing each verse ten

times and painstakingly choose the best takes from each version, to make sure we ended up with the most perfect result possible, every time.

I was proud of what I'd achieved, but I didn't want to take anything for granted, in case things went wrong. If this album bombed I knew I'd be completely devastated, regardless of the success of the single. I couldn't risk adding to any potential pain by feeling too self-satisfied or overly confident, because then I'd have further to fall. I was in a state of nervous anticipation every day, and in the middle of all this I was invited back on *The X Factor*, to perform 'Say You Won't Let Go', as Syco had discussed when they signed me up again. I'd wanted this chance for so long, but I was petrified when my big moment came.

I guess it was inevitable that being back in the chaos and intensity of *The X Factor* studio triggered major anxiety. I'd been asking myself for the past two years if it was possible to get back on that stage as part of my comeback. I'd envisioned this moment, just like Conor McGregor visualised becoming world champion of UFC within two years. Now everything I willed to happen was coming to fruition.

*Winning* The X Factor *was not the start of my career. This is. This is where it all starts.*

That's exactly how I felt and what I was telling myself. I hadn't been ready to take on that responsibility first time round. The weight of it was way too heavy for me, but now I had so much more strength and self-awareness, and I was up for the challenge.

I was very disappointed by my performance; I thought it was terrible. I sounded pitchy and I was so incredibly anxious I even got one of the lyrics wrong. Afterwards I went on

Twitter to apologise and explain it was the most nerve-racking thing I'd ever done. It was true. I'd wished for this moment for so long, and to perform my single in front of Simon and Nicole was too much. I still don't know how I got through it. It was like three years of emotions were coming out, and that night I had a very severe panic attack, on the balcony of my flat.

*Just breathe. You can do it. You've got it this time. You're strong enough. You can get through this.*

The reaction from the public was amazing; more than I could ever have wished for. People loved my performance, despite the glitches. Simon called me the 'comeback kid' and afterwards he sent me champagne and told me, 'Well done for doing it your way.' Now, finally, I was really starting to believe I'd pulled this whole thing off. I wasn't going to crash and burn this time, and my success wasn't going to fizzle out after one hit single either. I was back, to stay.

A few weeks later my album went to number one. I find it hard to put into words how that made me feel; the sense of achievement was phenomenal. The fact the record is so personal and honest made it all the more satisfying. Somebody called it the 'anti-*X Factor* album', because of lyrics like 'Did you see them build me up / Before I teared myself down'. The truth is I didn't write any of the songs to deliberately show *The X Factor* in a bad light. I don't blame *The X Factor* for anything. It's the opposite. It gave me a fantastic opportunity and I believe it was the path I was meant to take, even though I wasn't ready for it. I wrote *Back from the Edge* as my redemption and survival album, cataloguing what I'd been through over the past two years. I was super-proud of myself, and now I had all kinds of amazing opportunities opening up to me.

I was asked to take part in Radio 1's *Secret Busker*. I thought it was a great concept and I loved the fact I'd be judged purely on my voice and nothing else, so I jumped at the chance. I spent two hours in make-up being transformed into an old Scottish guy called 'Big Willy', and after performing at Waterloo station I raised more money for charity than Radio 1's professional busker band, which was the challenge. I loved winning, but most of all it was an extra bit of validation for me. I'd been wishing for years to have my music come before my reputation, and even though a lot of people sussed Big Willy out before the end of my busking session, I considered it a triumph.

My single was at number one for six weeks in Australia, and I was invited to their ARIA Music Awards in the November. I felt so honoured to be on the red carpet, especially when I looked up and saw Robbie Williams on the opposite side, giving an interview. He spotted me, stopped what he was doing and darted over to give me a massive hug.

'Mate, wow! What the hell have you achieved? It's unbelievable!'

'Thank you so much! Wow, mate!'

'Honestly, I'm so proud and impressed. You're phenomenal.'

Robbie knew how much I rated him. I'd told him when he mentored me on X Factor, and I'd tweeted about him many times, saying he's the best example of a performer imaginable, as that's what I firmly believe. Robbie told me he'd seen my tweets and thanked me. It was wild; I was playing on the same pitch as Robbie now – how had my life turned around like this?

At Christmas I went home to Redcar and bought everyone in the family a really cool present. It wasn't about being flash,

I just wanted to see all their faces light up. I'd felt guilty the previous year when I couldn't treat them as I wanted to, because I'd lost all my money. I felt I'd let everybody down and I hated the fact I'd caused so much grief in recent years for the people I loved. Seeing the pleasure on their faces was an important part of my comeback; it was another brick in my foundations being set back in place.

I got sick with a bug while I was up there. I guess it was partly a reaction to everything I'd been through in the previous few months, and I just needed to stop and recharge my mind and body. I ended up spending two weeks watching all six series of *Game of Thrones*, eating crap and getting fat. It was just what I needed; believe it or not, watching that series is up there as one of the best experiences of my life.

Going back to Redcar always brings out a mixture of emotions in me. I like the nostalgic smell of the seaside and having familiar places and faces around me. I've felt so lost and lonely in London, and it's so comforting to be on my home turf, but I also experience a sinking feeling sometimes, whenever I remember how down I was for so many years. It might grip me when I drive past Tesco or Somerfield, and I have a vivid flashback.

*I can't sleep because I'm so hungry. Will there ever be a time when I don't have to steal for my dinner every day?*

Occasionally I remember things that have been buried so deep I haven't thought of them for years, and disturbing memories like that set my nerves on edge and drag my mood down. Having said that, I have no regrets about things that happened to me growing up, because I believe everything I've been through, as a boy and as a man, has shaped the person I am today. I'm also super-proud of where I come from, and I like the fact that when I'm in some surreal celebrity situation I can laugh at myself and keep my feet on the ground, like most northerners.

I was invited on *The Late Late Show with James Corden* in the New Year, and that was definitely one of those crazy showbiz moments. It was my US TV debut, and James introduced me by saying I was the biggest-selling British artist of 2016.

'So thrilled for all your success. Incredible!' James said.

I honestly didn't know what to say. There I was in LA, on this legendary TV show being interviewed by a guy I'd admired for years. I genuinely wanted to go, 'No, mate, you must have made some mistake. You've got the wrong guy. I'm James Arthur, from Redcar.'

That interview heralded the start of a super-busy year for me, and not just with my music. After that I had an operation on my nose, to straighten it out after all the scraps I'd been in over the years. The shape of my nose had started to affect my breathing and my voice, so I wanted to get it sorted out once and for all.

The op went fine but while I was still recovering from the surgery, the trial came up of the guy who glassed me on the back of the head six months earlier. His name was Christopher Revell, and I'd learned he attacked me because I'd previously slept with his ex-girlfriend, and he thought I'd smirked at him that night in the pub. The reality was I didn't know who he was or what he looked like, and I wouldn't have smirked at him even if I did.

Revell claimed he'd only punched me and didn't attack me with a glass, but I had witnesses and evidence to prove exactly what happened. Even though I looked like an idiot with the plasters still on my nose from the surgery, I was determined to show up in court and make sure the truth came out. It emerged that Revell had a history of battery and assault, and he was jailed for five and a half years after pleading guilty to wounding with intent.

I wish none of it had happened. We both got a long sentence. I still feel traumatised today, not only by the idea I need to be on my guard in my home town in case I am attacked again, but by the thought my head injury might have repercussions for my mental health in years to come. I can't help feeling like that. Fundamentally I am still a nervous and paranoid person. I've read a lot about how head injuries can cause long-term damage and I can't delete that knowledge. I believe I'll always have to be vigilant.

In March I was finally back on stage, exactly where I wanted to be, doing my first UK tour in three years. It was a sell-out, and I loved every single show. 'Say You Won't Let Go' – which had been nominated for two Brit Awards – went double platinum. It was a lot to take in. I'd look at the framed record in my flat and wonder if I was imagining it. It was so unbelievable that my hopes and dreams had come true to this extent. My comeback was being described in the media as 'epic'. I couldn't get over how quickly my life had turned around.

Every day I was waking up and feeling stunned all over again. It was what I'd done after I'd won *The X Factor*, but back then, when I realised I wasn't dreaming and this was my reality, I panicked. I'll never forget it.

*What do I do, what do I do? Shit! I'll just close my eyes and go back to sleep. I don't want anything to do with this.*

Now it was very different. Every morning when I opened my eyes and realised the dream was real I felt so incredibly grateful, and I wanted to look after what I had, and strive for more success.

*This is insane. How many people get a second chance like this, a break that is even better than the first? I never want this to end.*

I told myself to appreciate every moment I was living, and that is what I am trying to do, every single day, on every level. When I can go to the shop and look the assistant in the eye I feel proud of myself, and when I stand on a stage and hold an audience for an hour and a half, I give myself credit.

It isn't always easy. I still suffer from panic attacks and acute anxiety, and that's something I have to manage all the time. I performed 'Say You Won't Let Go' on *The Tonight Show* with Jimmy Fallon, which felt like the pinnacle of my whole career. It's such a famous show and reaches more than three million Americans coast to coast. Jimmy's a superstar, and he announced me by saying, 'Tonight's musical guest has produced a massive international hit. It has been streamed one billion times worldwide. Wow. Well done!' Earlier on Danny DeVito had come into my dressing room to say hello and tell me he loved my music. It's the stuff of dreams – more than I could ever have dreamed of, in fact. It's also enough to test the mettle of the most fearless and self-possessed person, which is why I have to be super-vigilant, every single day.

I need to keep a very close eye on myself, but knowing that is half the battle. I can spot the triggers and the temptations. I know the voices of the demons and I recognise the spaces in between. I've learned so much about myself and how to deal with my issues and, because of everything I've been through, I'm much closer to knowing who I am.

I hope my story might help other people with anxiety and

mental health issues, because if I can get through, in the spotlight and with strangers judging and scrutinising me, I honestly think anyone can.

Going back to the boy has been one of the hardest things I've ever done, but it has also been uplifting. I'm so grateful for where I am now, and if I can inspire others, it has been worth the effort.

# Notes on mental health and happiness

We're all on a different path and maybe we all need to go back to the boy, or to the girl, to find our way to happiness. Navigating mental health is hard. I've struggled so much but I've learned so much too, about how to deal with my addictions and depression, panic attacks and anxiety issues.

I've made a lot of notes to myself over the years, about what I've found out and what works for me. I'm sharing them here, in case they might be helpful to anyone else.

## What I've learned about my habits and addictions

### Prescription drugs

I've done a lot of research into the antidepressants I've taken in the past and I don't believe there is enough concrete evidence to prove how they work and how effective they are. In my case, antidepressants did help me at times, but ultimately I feel they made me too paranoid. I hated the stigma and I believe I got addicted to the feeling of them taking away all my problems, when they were actually causing more. I was numb and felt I was always living 'in the middle'. I worry the pills altered my mind and that I've never been the same since, because it took me such a long time to stand on my own two feet after coming off them. I wish I had seen them as more of a temporary solution than I did, and that I'd paired them with other things rather than being overly reliant on them. If I had my time again I'd try therapy first before antidepressants, sleeping pills or tranquillisers. I did try therapy once but I didn't connect with the therapist and felt I couldn't let my guard down. This was partly because of my trust issues. I should have tried someone else, and this is something I'd still consider doing now I'm in a good place, to help keep me here.

## Smoking

I smoked on and off ever since I had my first 'rollies' with my mates when I was fifteen. Smoking helped me stay calm when I was taking drugs and when I was coming off the antidepressants. I always smoked more on a night out when I was drinking, and that's when I found it hard to stop. I didn't realise for years how much damage I was doing by smoking tobacco along with weed. The paramedic who educated me about adrenaline dumps taught me that the nicotine in tobacco initially causes a fast release of adrenaline, which makes the heart beat faster and can cause rapid, shallow breathing. Clearly that does not help a person like me who suffers from anxiety and panic attacks. I now hate the smell of cigarettes and smoking feels dirty to me. It was easy to give up when I realised it wasn't good for my voice on top of everything else. Even so, I am still tempted on a night out; that's addiction for you.

### Other drugs

I wanted to do anything that would take me out of reality. I thought I had nothing to lose and wanted to experiment. In fact drugs brought out demons and made me narcissistic. There was minimal comedown the next day, but weaning myself off those drugs for good was super-hard. I suffered horrible withdrawal symptoms and felt I couldn't function, which made me take more antidepressants and smoke more weed. I wish I'd never done those drugs, and I worry about what damage I have done to my brain because I've never been as mentally sharp since.

### Alcohol

I've never had a major problem with alcohol in moderation. I avoid spirits and mixing my drinks and I have to be careful not to overdo it, because if I drink too much I reach the point of blackout and lose chunks of time from my memory. Then I spend the next few days feeling super-anxious, fearing I've offended someone, or that I looked ridiculous. Again, it's about knowing when to stop, and reminding myself of the consequences of having one too many.

### Sex

For me, sex is healthy, good for the ego, self-esteem and it gives a natural buzz. As long as I'm respectful, safe and protected I can't see any downside, but of course it's very different when I'm in a relationship. I never want to hurt someone who loves me and I know it's not good enough to say the sex doesn't mean anything.

## Gambling

I understand that I need to do my research and be calculating and measured if I'm going to gamble. I've learned there is such a thing as 'angry betting', and if I were to put on a bet when my head wasn't straight it would be dangerous. The same goes for betting in a rush. If I have a bet now, I give myself a set amount of money, I do my homework, I take my time and I know when to walk away from the table. I also remind myself there is no such thing as a safe bet . . . well, not unless Floyd Mayweather is fighting a little guy!

## *What I've learned about my depression*

I know I am suffering from serious depression when I hear a lot of noise in my head and scary, negative voices. I see terrifying things, like visions of myself dropping dead. When I talk to myself to try to rationalise what is happening so many other voices come in, taking the piss out of me. They ask me what the point of my life is and why am I talking to myself. They torment me, saying I must be crazy. I convince myself I am not like everyone else. I feel so different and I am terrified of appearing mad to other people. I don't want to see anyone and I don't want anyone to look at me. I want to shut myself away. That's when I know things are bad.

My depression always deepens when I feel I have transgressed and I am disappointed in myself. Those feelings validate what the demons in my head are saying. Appearing vulnerable in front of other people also pulls me down. I show my vulnerability sometimes because I think it helps other people, but then I get annoyed with myself and think what I've done is a blessing and a curse. I regret it for days afterwards. I know I care way too much about what other people think of me; that is my main issue. I overthink how other people feel about me, and when you are in the spotlight, that overthinking takes over and is so hard to switch off.

When I feel desperately low I envisage myself leaving this world, usually by thinking about jumping off something. I have a strategy for curbing suicidal feelings. I think of the people who care about me, and most of all I think about my sisters. My little sister Neve suffers from anxiety and panic attacks and Sian and Jazz both have issues with anxiety. I make myself think, 'If you did this, Neve might think she could.' It's such a strong and shocking idea and it reminds me I could never do it, not ever.

## Things that help me with panic attacks

- Recognising triggers. For me these are being in hotel rooms, getting in the bath and anything to do with *The X Factor*. I keep an extra eye on myself when I am exposed to those triggers.

- Being aware of the signs and trying to regulate my breathing as soon as I feel anxious and can't breathe normally.

- Taking deep breaths.

- Taking myself to a place where I am safe, and away from anyone who might make my anxiety worse.

- Letting someone I love be there to help me.

- Going outside and breathing fresh air.

- Taking a long walk.

- Running as fast as I can, to give my heart a reason to beat so fast.

- Giving myself a slap in the face, or a hard smack.

- Splashing water on my face.

- Having a paramedic's number in my phone, for reassurance, or talking to any medical professional.

## Things that help with my anxiety

*Mindfulness* I try to have a quiet moment with myself and mentally go to a place where I can remember being happy. I think of standing in the sea in Thailand, feeling connected to the planet. I remember paradise; looking back at the beach and the palm trees.

*Appreciating simple things.* I like stepping out of my everyday world and just walking the earth, wherever that may be. I enjoy the feeling of not having anywhere to be, living a simple life, eating good natural food and just being.

*Staying in the now.* The past has been and gone, and trying to control it only causes regret and guilt. I know I can't control what is going to happen tomorrow, and if I try it will only make me anxious and fearful. All I can control is what is in front of me right now. It's difficult to master, but I'm learning to be the watcher of my thoughts and to ask myself 'How is this making me feel, right now?'

*Trying to have rational, positive thoughts* that trump the negative voices in my head, and having a strategy for picking off irrational thoughts. I focus on breathing and tell myself that respiration runs deeper than anxiety: breathing is my power.

*Writing songs.* It's super-therapeutic for me. When the words sound real I'm very, very happy. Music is my ultimate coping mechanism and medicine. I'd be lost without it.

*Following my heart.* In the past I wasted too much time worrying about what other people thought and wanted. I've finally learned to listen to myself more, and do what feels real and natural to me. It takes the pressure off.

*Eating less dairy and gluten.* I don't think I have a medical intolerance and I would not give up any food group completely without talking to a doctor, but I know dairy and gluten make me feel clogged up and bloated, which brings my mood down and makes me feel sluggish and disappointed with myself.

*Eating cashew nuts,* avocados, blueberries, green vegetables – all good for the brain and body.

*Avoiding caffeine,* junk food, fizzy drinks and alcohol. I always dip or crash afterwards and it can take me days to recover. I haven't drunk coffee in years.

*Going vegetarian,* after talking to an expert and making sure it was safe and healthy for me. The more I learn about farming methods, the more eating meat bothers me. Eating veggie is not just good for my physical health, it makes me feel better about myself as a living creature on the planet.

*Drinking plenty of water.* I spent a lot of years being dehydrated and not realising how it contributed to headaches and irritability.

*Taking Probio7.* It's a probiotic nutritional supplement the guys in my band introduced me to. It contains 'friendly bacteria' and seems to help my digestive system, which makes me feel better.

*Exercising hard,* especially if I've lapsed and had a heavy week-end, which I do occasionally (I think we all need a blowout from time to time, though I always regret it afterwards). I have a proper sweat session, running on a treadmill and working out on a boxing machine to flush out the toxins. I can feel it working and it lifts my mood immediately.

*Sleeping well and avoiding being nocturnal.* I'm not very good at this as I've always been a night owl (it's why I have an owl tattoo on my neck). My problem is switching off the mindless chatter in my head. Getting up early, even if I'm shattered, filling my day and being productive always helps, and then my mind is worn out when I want to sleep.

*Minding the spaces in between.* I know I am vulnerable when I have too much time on my hands or am in a gap of any kind. We all need time to chill and do nothing, but I have to be extra-vigilant at those times, and make sure I don't dwell on negatives or fret about the future.

*Reading and learning about mental health* and how to achieve happiness. I like *The Power of Now* by Eckhart Tolle, *The Alchemist* by Paulo Coelho, *Happy* by Derren Brown and *Feel the Fear and Do It Anyway* by Susan Jeffers.

*Talking.* I've found it cathartic and therapeutic to open up and tell my story. Talking to trusted friends and family members helps me put things in perspective.

*Giving.* Being an ambassador for Sane makes me feel I am part of something useful, and serving the community in some way. It's rewarding and uplifting and reminds me I am not worthless; I have something to contribute.

*Staying connected with people,* even when I feel like hiding myself away. Isolation causes more anxiety.

*Visualisation.* If you can think it, you can achieve it. I visualised being successful in music and I managed to hold it in my hands. I'm happy now, and I want to hold onto that. I can see myself happy in the future, and that is the best antidote to anxiety there is.

# Epilogue

Since I went on *The Tonight Show* with Jimmy Fallon, I've reached more milestones and had so many phenomenal experiences.

'Say You Won't Let Go' has had over two billion streams. The single is multi-platinum worldwide, it made the billboard top ten and went to number one on the US Radio Airplay Chart.

I've played to an electrifying crowd of 80,000 at Capital's Summertime Ball and I got head-to-toe goosebumps at the Radio 1's Big Weekend, when tens of thousands of people sang my songs back to me. I've done a European tour and I've performed at concerts all over America, sharing the bill with global artists. By the time this book is published I will have toured the US with OneRepublic and I'll be about to embark on my first UK arena tour.

It's all mind-blowing, shivers-down-the spine stuff, but the best thing of all is that I've become more calm and centred, despite being flat-out busy. I feel the most settled I've ever been in my life, and I have never been happier. Amazingly, I've done it on my own, without the help of therapy or psychiatry, and I'm doing so well with absolutely no crutches. It's just me and my mind, and I am not even feeling the pressure. I've come a very long way, and I am so proud of myself.

Writing this book has been incredibly therapeutic. It felt like I grew up while I was working on it and, when I read it back, it was as if everything clicked into place. It's been tough remembering what I was like as a boy, and how I felt, but it's been worth the pain because I've learned so much. I'm shocked at how many times words like misfit, oddball and weirdo came into my mind, but they were part of my daily vocabulary for so long I couldn't avoid them. Now I'm so much more positive, and I am trying to change my language and use words like eccentric, unique and individual instead. I have a much healthier perspective on life.

Describing the darkest moments and the panic attacks triggered my anxiety several times, but I wanted to go into all the detail I have, to hopefully raise awareness and help other people who may be suffering. The process has helped me: I'm now able to beat off anxiety attacks in a minute. I do it by having a little word with myself when I feel the signs. *Why are you stressed about having dinner in this restaurant, with these people? You're just eating food. It's fuel, so you can go for a run later. You'll feel absolutely amazing once you get on the treadmill, and then you will go to bed and feel calm and content.*

I wish I'd learned that technique years ago. If I could go back in time I'd tell myself to put things in context much more than I ever did; to remember what the plot is and not get skewered by the minutiae of daily life. Some of the things that triggered my anxiety seem almost laughable now. Looking back, I found myself wanting to tell my younger self off, and say, 'What the heck is all this fuss about, James? It really isn't as bad as you think it is. You seriously can't be having yet another meltdown! Think about what you will do next, when you leave this stressful situation. Come on, man!' Instead I was masking my issues with medication and weed, thinking I was dealing with them when really I was doing anything but.

I can see now that I used to internalise things way too much, and I realise how much better I've become at speaking my mind and expressing myself. I've also re-learned how vital my music is to me, in terms of how I need it to channel my emotions and stay happy and positive. I didn't always recognise that. When I had to sell my guitars to survive I didn't appreciate the effect it would have on my mental health, but I do now.

I need to be more forgiving towards my parents. The world does not revolve around me. I am more understanding of what life was like for my mum and my dad when I was a boy, and I forgive them for everything. Mum has come back from the brink as well, and I admire how far she has come. She is a great mum and a fantastic person, and she is in a very good place now. There is nobody on planet earth who understands me like she does; we are connected, and she is the first person I would call if ever I went into a dark place again. I know that is possible and I know I need to be vigilant, because having depressive tendencies is part of me and how I am built.

I'm still growing and maturing, and life is really exciting. I have new goals and dreams. The success I'm having has given me my confidence back and made me want to be more content with my physical appearance. Like so many people, I want to look in the mirror and be happy with the shape I am in, and I'm on track to achieve that. I know I can.

Acting is a big ambition. Remembering how happy I was on stage as a boy makes me want a piece of that again. I'd also like to spend more time in LA, where I've been working on my music with some of the biggest names in the industry. I love the sunshine and the relaxed lifestyle in California. It's so easy to be vegetarian and there are beautiful hikes to go on. I could never leave the UK for good. I'm very British at heart and I'd miss my family and friends too much, and the seasons. But it's liberating to have choices, now my career is back on track. I feel permanently on the edge of the next great thing, but at the same time my focus is on enjoying and appreciating what I am doing now, in this moment.

I want my next album to be less personal and self-indulgent than the last one. It's all about the music this time; it's for other people. This book is for others too. I would not have shared my life story for the sake of it, just for me. I've done it because I've read books about anxiety and depression that I've identified with and benefitted from.

I hope my book will be helpful for any other eccentric, unique and individual people out there. No weirdos allowed!

# Acknowledgements

Firstly, thank you to my family for letting me speak so openly and honestly about our lives. Especially my mum Shirley Ashworth and my dad Neil Arthur. I love you both very much.

My sisters, Sian, Jazz, Neve and Charlotte, my brother Neil. Dad's wife Jackie, and all my aunties and uncles and cousins in Glasgow.

Special thanks to Jessica Grist. You know what you have done for me.

Thank you for the music! And of course for my loyal fans. Without you, who knows where I would be.

Thanks to my publishers, Hodder & Stoughton, for giving me the opportunity to tell my story exactly how I wanted to. Thanks to my editor Briony Gowlett, editorial assistant Cameron Myers and literary agent Rory Scarfe.

Rachel Murphy, my ghostwriter. I can't believe how perceptively and accurately you've written this, how therapeutic the process has been and how easy you have made it for me. I could not be happier with my book, and that is down to you.

James Grant Management. You have been truly phenomenal, backing me when nobody else dared. I am so grateful to Neil Rodford, Martin Hall, Michael Hall and Helen Gilliat. All your pep talks helped keep my chin up when the chips were down. Helen, you have given me the best daily support a northerner like me could wish for! You all continue to help me keep my head straight.

Russell Eslamifar, what can I say? You had my back even before I realised I needed rescuing. Thank you for bringing me on board at James Grant and for always believing in me. You have been a fantastic support and have helped me so much with all my work in the US lately. I can't thank you enough.

My touring party, JP Firmin and Meg McKenzie, Dan Bingham (my MD) and all the boys in the band deserve an extra special mention, for sticking with me from the start. It's been an amazing ride, with a lot more to come.

A massive thank you to Sony Germany for your belief in me and for making this record happen! Willy Ehmann, Phillip Ginthoer, Stefan Goebel, Bene Vonstauffenberg, Lena Gerecke and of course my amazing A&R Ina Jedlicka. Big love to you all.

Simon Cowell, Sonny Takhar, Tyler Brown and all the Syco team for helping make my new venture work since being re-signed by Syco.

To my US label Columbia for making my American dream come true. Thank you Rob Stringer, Joel Klaiman, Matt Amoroso, Lee Leipsner, Jon Borris, Pete Cosenza, Kim Harris and Catherine McNelly. 'Say You Won't Let Go' has now gone triple platinum in the US!

To CAA and SJM who kept my live shows and touring going even when it was tough. Andy Pountain, Paul Fitzgerald, Emma Banks, Brian Manning, Lee Goforth and Simon Moran.

A special thank you to my amazing lawyer Talya Sheldon who works above and beyond for me, always.

My mates from back home. Danny McCauley, Michael Dawson, Jamie Graham, Michael Petite and Paul Gill. You keep my feet on the ground. You *are* home.

Tom Laverick, a good friend of mine who has cerebral palsy. We spent a lot of time together, and helping care for you gave me a purpose before I went on *The X Factor*.

All the lads I've ever been in bands with, particularly Josh Newell-Brown, Karl Dowson, Alex Beer, Travis Shaw, Matthew Green, Jordan Swain, Chris Smalls, Jez Taylor and Nathan Futo. Thanks also to Rich Doney and John McGough for helping me get my music together in the early years.

Dan White, my old touring manager, and Luke Higgins, who helped me do the gigs that kept me out of the red after I lost my way.

My fantastic team on *The X Factor*: Annabel, Ian, Graham and Gavo. Also Nicole Scherzinger, Gary Barlow, Tulisa, Louis Walsh, Jahméne and Rylan, for being kind, supportive, sympathetic and so encouraging during that mind-blowing journey. You all raised my spirits and helped keep me in the game when I was struggling.

Magna, my janitor! You came to do the cleaning but looked after me, as well as my flat. You're a good friend, and you bring me positive energy. Thank you.

All the global radio stations that supported my comeback. You put me on the A list and played my new music on rotation. You gave me a second chance; I think we all deserve that. THANK YOU.

Finally, thank you to all the hundreds of paramedics who 'saved my life'. Even though I was not dying, you really did bring me back from the edge. Thank you. Without you, this could have been a very different story.

# Picture Acknowledgements

The author and publisher would like to thank the following copyright-holders for permission to reproduce images in this book:

©FremantleMedia/Simco Ltd: Chapters 8, 10 and 14
©Gary Walsh Photography: Chapter 4
©James Grant Group Ltd: Chapter 24
©Katie Tweddle: Chapter 21
©Ray Tang/REX/Shutterstock: Chapter 12
©Rylan Clark-Neal: Chapter 6
©Sony Music: Chapter 22
©Syco/Rahul Bhatt: Chapter 18

All other images are care of the author

The author and publishers have made all reasonable efforts to contact copyright-holders for permission, and apologise for any omissions or errors in the form of credit given. Corrections may be made to future printings.

### An invitation from the publisher

Join us at www.hodder.co.uk, or follow us
on Twitter @hodderbooks to be a part of
our community of people who love the very
best in books and reading.

Whether you want to discover more about a book
or an author, watch trailers and interviews, have the
chance to win early limited editions, or simply browse
our expert readers' selection of the very best books,
we think you'll find what you're looking for.

And if you don't, that's the place to tell us what's missing.

**We love what we do, and we'd love you to be a part of it.**

www.hodder.co.uk

@hodderbooks

HodderBooks

HodderBooks